MOVIE LOT TO BEACHHEAD

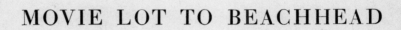

MOVIE LOT TO BEACHHEAD

THE MOTION PICTURE GOES TO WAR

AND PREPARES FOR THE FUTURE

by the EDITORS OF LOOK

With a Preface by ROBERT ST. JOHN

DOUBLEDAY, DORAN AND COMPANY, INC.

GARDEN CITY   1945   NEW YORK

PREFACE

There was a day when it was considered smart to be cynical about Hollywood.

That was before the war.

That was before American newsreels proved, indisputably, with footage from abroad, what some newspaper correspondents and radio commentators were trying to say about the evil powers at loose in the world.

That was before Hollywood cameramen packed up their tripods and went off to photograph war—and to write an unsurpassed chapter of personal daring and bravery.

That was before so many screen stars changed their spats and their walking sticks for uniforms and guns.

That was before many of Hollywood's glamour girls, who seemed so frail and willowy, rode unheated transport planes and dirty jeeps to entertain, on remote islands, men hungry for just that touch of home.

That was before the U. S. Army and Navy began to use men from the studios, the script rooms and movie lots to make films to train raw recruits in ways of fighting a war.

That was before filmdom began to turn out documentaries to be distributed abroad, designed to prove to the rest of the world (friends and foes alike) that this is a land of democracy and freedom and opportunity for all manner of men.

That was before Hollywood started making feature pictures about the war which (fictional though they were) brought some of the truths of war home to America more graphically than any of the cold little facts which people read in their papers.

When Hollywood went to war, Hollywood became mature and began to win the respect of those who had been the most cynical toward it.

We war correspondents, who have seen all these activities of Hollywood folk abroad, are today among the most respectful. We can vouch for the truth of what the pages of this book portray.

But, to me, the most exciting chapter of the book is the final one, "Epilogue to War."

After the shooting stops, after the stars and starlets, the cameramen and script writers return to the movie lots, Hollywood naturally will go back to the business of making films strictly for profit. But it will also do something else. Now that Hollywood has grown up, it knows that it must play its role in creating the world of tomorrow, just as it helped to destroy the kind of world desired by the enemy.

To those with even a little imagination, this volume proves that here is an influence for good which planners of the postwar world will not dream of overlooking.

If there be any doubters, let them read the text and study the pictures which follow.

Robert St. John
January, 1945
New York City

CONTENTS

MOVIE LOT TO BEACHHEAD

CHAPTER I

PROLOGUE TO WAR

"Hollywood" is more than the name of a place. The word has many meanings. To movie-struck girls on Main Street it is a fairy land of the impossible come true; to its tired cynics with a knack of turning a phrase it is "the only insane asylum run by the inmates"; to critics of "escapist" entertainment it is "Graustark on the Pacific"; to a lucky few it is the end of the rainbow. And Hollywood is a great deal more.

Hollywood is a section of Los Angeles. It is headquarters for a two-billion-dollar world-wide industry that has made art and entertainment its business. That industry is "Hollywood." This book concerns itself with the part it has played, its motion pictures and theaters have played, in the second World War, and the part they will continue to play in the post-war world.

For years before the war, people in the moving picture industry worked and played hard. Their long hours in the studios, their interminable shoptalk, were as well known as the lavishness of their parties, the splendor of their premises, and the opulence of their swimming pools. Hollywood attended the races and bet huge sums; it played cards interminably. Its clothes were flamboyant, its manners informal. It went to premières amid batteries of searchlights, flanked by temporary grandstands.

Hollywood, the community, however, has much in common with other American communities; it is more like them than unlike. Long before Pearl Harbor one might have found in any American community a group of people who sensed the growing menace of Fascism and the coming of war. There was such a group in Hollywood, too, and there, as elsewhere, it grew steadily.

In fact, it grew a bit faster and sooner in Hollywood than in most American communities, for the motion picture industry's artists and technicians come from all nations and races, and before Pearl Harbor its pictures were produced for a world market. That market shrank as Fascist-minded countries began to bar American films.

In June, 1938, Walter Wanger produced *Blockade,* a picture dealing with the Spanish Civil War. The film did not identify the opposing forces, although its sympathies were clearly with the Loyalists. Mild as the picture was, it created a furore. Picketed in some cities and banned in others, it was not a box office success.

A year later Warner Brothers produced *Confessions of a Nazi Spy.* It was based on evidence presented at a trial of German spies in New York City's Federal District Court. The film charged that German-American Bunds were mills for espionage, sabotage and propaganda, that the German consulates were little more than cloaks for a hidden warfare against the United States.

The effect was electric. Actors and producers received murder threats. German Chargé d'Affaires Thomsen screamed "Conspiracy!" The picture was banned by many countries anxious not to offend Germany. In the United States, however, it made a profound impression.

As far back as 1934, *Judgment Day*, a play by Elmer Rice, had revealed the gangster methods of the Nazis. Public opinion polls reflected the American people's positive aversion to totalitarianism. What *Confessions of a Nazi Spy* said was nothing new. But the picture dramatized the dangers of Nazism, brought them vividly home to the American people. Isolationists began to charge Hollywood with being one-sided about the war in Europe. The charges mounted as more screen dramas told their stories against the backdrop of Nazi terror— *The Mortal Storm, Escape, Four Sons*.

Escape had been published in book form and as a magazine serial without any isolationist uproar. When MGM transferred the same story to film, however, the isolationists objected at the top of their lungs.

In the three years between Munich and our entrance into the war, Hollywood produced more than a thousand feature pictures. Fifty were anti-Nazi. For the bulk of its filmfare, the theater-going public preferred pictures more or less representative of American life, such as *Gone With the Wind, The Philadelphia Story, Mr. Smith Goes to Washington*.

But, from a small and highly vocal group of individuals, the fifty pictures brought the baseless charge that Hollywood was inciting the American people to war.

As 1941 drew to a close, a Senate subcommittee began an investigation of Hollywood's alleged "war mongering." Wendell Willkie, defending the industry, soon had the isolationists on the defensive. The investigation withered on the vine, although, just before Pearl Harbor, Senator Worth Clark announced that it would be resumed.

Between Hitler's attack on Poland and the Jap attack on Pearl Harbor, life in the film colony underwent a change. Hollywood had fun as usual. But it also thought and argued about the war. It raised funds for the USO, Russian War Relief, Greek War Relief, United China Relief, Bundles for Britain. Joan Crawford got $112,000 for making a picture and turned the check over to the Red Cross. Cary Grant split $100,000 between British and American war charities. Hundreds of studio workers—the great unsung of Hollywood—dug deep into their pockets and contributed to the War Chest.

ON THE MORNING of December 7, 1941, Hollywood bestirred itself late. It was a sparkling Sunday and there were many pleasant ways to fill the day. There were the beach at Malibu, the desert at Palm Springs, and the High Sierras, all within motoring range. It was a good day for tennis or golf or church. *The Great Dictator, Sergeant York* and *Citizen Kane* were playing in downtown Hollywood. Aimee Semple McPherson advertised two sermons for that day: *One Foot in Heaven* and *Keep 'em Flying*. Both were titles of current feature films.

Telephones began buzzing. The talk was about Harry Warner's new granddaughter; about the antiaircraft artillery men who had taken over Hollywood Park (but reporters were assured that the track would be open in time for the racing). People chatted about Saturday's auction of blooded cattle and the hot bidding by Gene Autry, Clark Gable and his wife, Carole Lombard; about Walter Huston's sprained ankle, and Eddie Albert's tonsils, just removed; about the camera crew that had been sent to Iceland to shoot Sonja Henie's next picture.

At 11:26 the stunning news flashed over the radio. Hollywood, like the rest of the country, sat back, dazed. Golfers returned to the clubhouse. Downtown, civilians and soldiers on leave gathered on street corners. Los Angeles' Little Tokyo looked like a deserted village.

Next day, Japanese employees in studios were told not to report for work until the Government had ruled on their status. They never returned.

One studio hastily shelved a planned musical called *Pearl Harbor Pearl*. Another dropped the title *I'll Take Manila*.

The prologue to war was over.

As most of the world knows, pre-war Hollywood was the land of super productions. A première, such as the one pictured above, was more than the first showing of a feature

film. It was a glittering spectacle with search-lights, microphones, carpets and richly dressed movie stars. Fans sat packed in grandstands for a glimpse of their idols.

Expensive sets, like this one, were built by the studios, used once and discarded. D. W. Griffith still holds the record for the colony's most expensive set. It cost $300,000.

William R. Hearst's castle, *San Simeon*, became the model for huge Hollywood estates.

In its leisure time, the movie colony was frivolous and gay. Parties were expensive.

Carefree, boisterous Hollywood played noisily and enjoyed its heated swimming pools.

Horses ran for the world's richest purse ($100,000) at near-by Santa Anita race track.

Hollywood's night life was in full swing and its stars were besieged for autographs.

On Sundays the moving picture colony amused itself by watching and playing polo.

True, Hollywood wasn't fun for everyone. It wasn't for mothers who waited in line each day nursing the scant hope that their children might one day become movie stars.

Celebrities enjoyed privacy only in their own homes. Here, a crowd presses against the windows of a restaurant in Venice (Hollywood's amusement park) to gape at a star.

A most popular star was Carole Lombard, wife of Clark Gable, who later lost her life on a bond-selling tour. Charming, witty, she made people laugh on and off the screen.

All Quiet on the Western Front, released by Universal in 1930, and taken from the novel by Erich Remarque, reflected the prevailing pacifism of the American people, their

disillusionment following the first World War, their feeling of war's futility. The pic- ture caused riots when it was exhibited in Germany and it was quickly suppressed.

Germany still dreamed war and revenge. Her hatred of the democracies crystallized when Hitler became Chancellor in 1933. He is shown with his ministers at Berchtesgaden.

In 1937 the Japanese attacked the Chinese near Peking and the Orient was in flames. Above is a newsreel picture recording the wanton slaughter of civilians in Nanking.

Late in 1938 Hollywood made its first anti-Fascist film—*Blockade*. Although the picture was but a mild indictment of the Fascists in Spain's Civil War, it caused a furore.

The totalitarian powers were marching against the civilized world—but the democ-racies failed to realize this. Hollywood's premières were as big and crowded as ever.

Sunset Strip, the night-club section of Holly-wood, was hilarious and bejeweled. And the customers laughed uproariously when a lady received a lump of ice down her back.

But the people of Europe were ceasing to laugh. Some countries were under attack, others feared it momentarily, and people of all nations prepared for coming disaster.

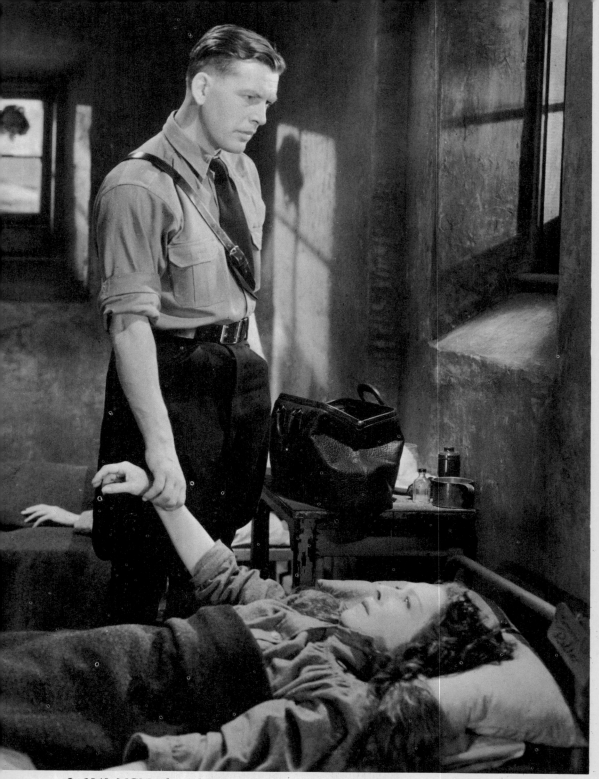

In 1940, MGM released *Escape* despite Nazi threats of a permanent ban on MGM pictures. The foreign market shrank, but Hollywood still continued to unmask Germany.

The Mortal Storm was released at the same time as *Escape,* under the same threat. MGM films were banned immediately in all Reich-controlled markets. War was drawing close.

Confessions of a Nazi Spy was an outspoken anti-Nazi film. This scene of a Bund meeting showed active sedition in the U. S. Hollywood was accused of "war mongering." The charge sounded ridiculous after Pearl Harbor when the F.B.I. released films . . .

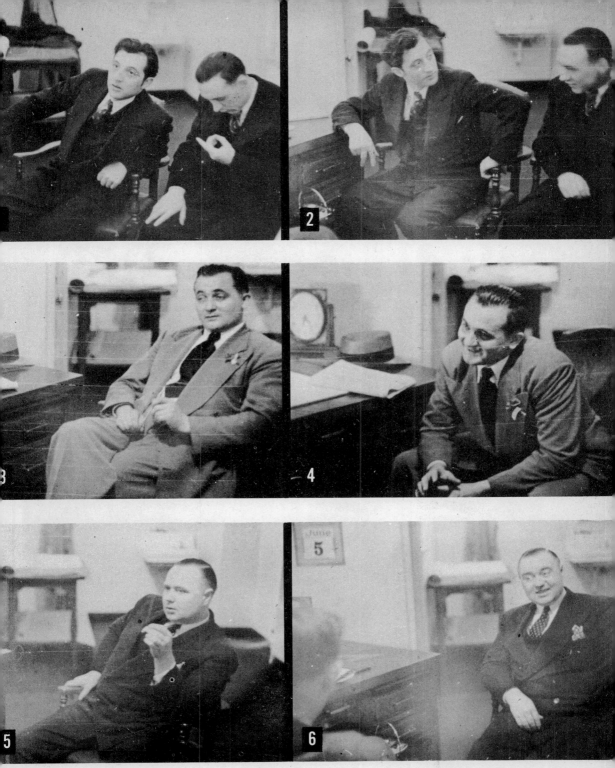

. . . used to gain convictions in a Federal court. Taken with a hidden camera, they showed a spy ring in America in actual oper- ation. Above, spies report and submit stolen blueprints to the master spy, Seabold (not in photos). Seabold, a G-man, trapped them all.

Meanwhile, Hollywood welcomed Europe's talented refugees. Typical was French-born René Clair, who left Europe after France fell, continued here as a successful director.

With war rolling toward these shores, Hollywood became more serious. It gave freely to war funds, visited training camps. Above, starlets accept a lift in a command car.

Backing the defense program, Hollywood's near-by aircraft and tank plants boomed.

Stars and lesser lights did volunteer relief duty for Britain, other war-torn countries.

The holocaust of Pearl Harbor galvanized America. As the thunder of Japanese bombs died away, the country found that it was united as never before. Forgotten were

the silly charges of Hollywood war mongering. Hollywood, along with the rest of the
nation, jumped to answer the call to arms,
freely yielding its sinew, blood and treasure.

CHAPTER II

NEWSREEL HISTORY

The newsreels found their voice just four years before Japan, in 1931, touched off the second World War with the invasion of Manchuria. Ours is the first generation able to see and hear history in the making.

For ten full years before Pearl Harbor, the screen had dramatized portentous happenings, caught by those recorders of modern history, the newsreel cameramen. Since then world-shaking events in Europe and in the Pacific have been re-enacted upon the screens of thousands of American theaters. International conferences at Casablanca, Moscow, Teheran, have come to our neighborhood movie houses. Guns have barked at many a small-town movie where today's grim-faced American servicemen once kicked and squirmed on their seats and whistled at Bill Hart and Douglas Fairbanks, in happy ignorance of the fact that one day they themselves would be the actors in history's greatest drama.

Adolf Hitler became Chancellor of Germany in 1933; newsreels covered the ceremony, with its hint of thunder and bloodshed to come. As the Axis pattern of conquest unfolded, almost every significant development appeared on moving film.

Mussolini's grab of Ethiopia, 1936 . . . . the Spanish civil war . . . . the Rome-Berlin Axis . . . . Japan's undeclared war in China . . . . Hitler's rape of Austria, 1938 . . . .

Munich . . . . Hitler's rape of Czechoslovakia . . . . Hitler's rape of Poland, 1939 . . . . the British and French declarations of war . . . . Hitler's rape of Denmark, Norway, Holland, Belgium, Luxembourg, France, Yugoslavia, Greece . . . . the Battle of Britain, 1940 . . . . the invasion of Russia, 1941. . . .

Since Pearl Harbor four-fifths of newsreel footage has dealt with some aspect of this total war. Newsreel cameras have accompanied bombers and fighters on thousand-plane raids; roved the Pacific with our naval task forces; portrayed historic landings in Africa, Italy and Normandy; revealed events of immense significance—raids on Tokyo, war in China, battles in the malarial slime of Jap-infested islands.

If all the newsreel footage shown since Pearl Harbor were spliced together, it would make more than a hundred feature-length films.

Each year 520 reels constitute the screen's news columns. The March of Time and the documentary film are its illustrated feature section. Some of the war's best documentaries have been composed almost exclusively of newsreel footage.

Visual information of such consequence, in such quantity, and dedicated to the truth, can be, and has been, of tremendous value in creating an informed public opinion. In the Axis nations, however, the newsreels became simply an instrument of propaganda. To movie-goers in those nations (and wherever else Axis films could find a market), dictator-controlled newsreels began expounding the virtues of Fascism, the joys of armed force, the obligation of master races to murder their neighbors. After Hitler's conquest of the Low Countries and France, European neutrals were shown *Sieg im Westen (Victory in the West)*, a brutal visualization of what happened to those who resisted Germany. It was exhibited in the guise of a documentary news film.

No such perversion of the newsreels occurred in America or in countries where native cameramen were employed by any of the five big American newsreel companies (Fox Movietone, News of the Day, Paramount, Pathe, Universal). The men who pictured events for American audiences were devoted to facts. For example:

In 1935, when Mussolini launched his mechanized assault on the tribesmen of Ethiopia, Universal News (among other companies) sent a cameraman — Howard Winner—to the scene. One day Italian fliers bombed a Swedish Red Cross unit at the southern frontier. All war correspondents had been confined to Addis Ababa, the capital, but Winner convinced Emperor Haile Selassie that, lacking visual proof to the contrary, the world would think the bombing story simply propaganda. The Negus lent Winner his private plane to go film the results of the bombing.

During the civil war in Spain (1936-39), our Government would not let American cameramen cover the action. Paramount News, however, employed a Russian named John Dored to film European events; he became the only cameraman representing an American company in Spain. Working behind the Loyalist lines, he was eventually captured by Franco's troops and released only after diplomatic exchanges.

In December, 1937, six months after Japan invaded China proper, 14 Americans were moved from the air-target city of Nanking to the protection of the ancient United States gunboat *Panay.* Among them were two newsreel cameramen—Norman Alley of Universal and Eric Mayell of Fox Movietone —who were in China to cover the undeclared war. When Japanese bombers deliberately sank the *Panay,* the two cameramen recorded the whole episode.

When Japanese "incidents" reached an infamous climax with the attack on Pearl Harbor, many newsreel men enlisted or were drafted into our armed services as combat photographers (see Chapter VI). Service-made footage, released through commercial theaters, soon became a major means of public information concerning the war. Some newsmen, however, remained civilians. Many were given war assignments that involved glory and deadly peril. As witness:

Fred Baylis of Paramount, after covering the German invasion of France and losing all his equipment at Dunkirk, was transferred to the Mediterranean. There, assigned to record the Allied landings in Sicily, he was starting off by air when his plane caught fire. Baylis was burned to death.

Earle Crotchett of Universal, filming operations in the South Pacific, was caught in a Japanese air raid on a New Guinea base. He broke his leg—but "caught" the raid.

Dave Oliver of Pathe News helped picture the advance of the Allied Fifth Army in Italy. During one engagement he skipped clear of a foxhole a few seconds before a German shell struck it, killing seven men.

Gaston Madru, a cameraman in Paris for News of the Day, buried film when the Germans entered the city in 1940. Later he went into the French underground movement. When American cameramen entered liberated Paris in 1944, they found Madru riding around on a captured German camera car with a sign—in English, for some reason!— "Please Don't Kill the French Cameramen." Snipers' bullets were still whining.

Damien Parer of Paramount News was almost continuously assigned to war coverage from Pearl Harbor to the Marine landings on Palau in September, 1944. He was killed by enemy machine gun fire while photographing front line operations.

Such stories point up the outstanding war and prewar record of the newsreel cameramen. They prove that these roving reporters are fighting for a freedom America should cherish: Freedom of the Screen.

Prophecy in celluloid, portent captured by the camera—here, in a picture taken in Nazi Germany in the mid-'30s, is grim warning of tragedy to come. At left stands Adolf Hitler, self-made ruler of the *Reich*, arm outstretched in savage benediction to his marching Storm Troopers. With such human machines he dreams of conquering the world.

In front of his car, cameramen record the prophetic scene; here and throughout Hitler's ascendant years, photographers were always present. Thus, even when German propaganda screamed loudest of Hitler's "peace aims," the camera was witness to reality: goose-stepping men, hard Nazi faces, the evil will of one man shaping history.

Across the world from Germany, Japan also planned for world dominion. Testimony to her methods is in this famous sequence of a Chinese baby, orphaned and rescued within a few minutes during the bombing of Shanghai in 1937. It was taken by H. S. ("Newsreel") Wong (above, at left), a Chinese cameraman working for News of the Day.

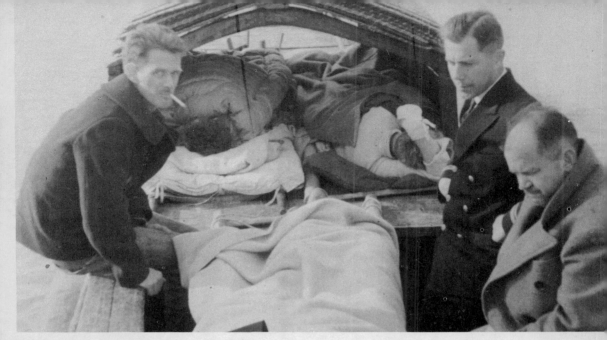

When Japanese bombers sank the gunboat U.S.S. *Panay* near Nanking, China, late in 1937, two American newsreel men were aboard. Heedless of risk, they photographed the attack. Later they filmed the removal of survivors (above). Their pictures were rushed to Washington, and quickly released —an unheeded warning—to the public.

Third piece in the mosaic of Axis aggression was Italy's invasion of Ethiopia in 1935. Here, while newsreel cameras turned, Emperor Haile Selassie vainly begged the League of Nations for aid, and the world heard the ominous, prophetic question of the Negus: "Are the States going to set up the terrible precedent of bowing before force?"

Civil war in Spain (1936-39), with each side receiving support from other nations, was also a dark prologue to global conflict, as newsreels showed. In this sequence, caught by a Fascist Italian cameraman, a Loyalist soldier stands to hurl a hand grenade into a Rebel trench; a rifle bullet drops him, but the grenade kills three of his enemies.

When Britain's Prime Minister Neville Chamberlain flew back from the Munich meeting with Hitler, Mussolini and Daladier, he stepped before the newsreel camera to speak reassuringly of Anglo-German "understanding" and "peace in our time." Hitler waited six months, then seized all Czechoslovakia and a year later attacked Poland.

Another British Premier, Winston Churchill, reaping the harvest Chamberlain sowed, dedicated his land to "Blood, sweat and tears." Through the camera's lens, American audiences learned the horrors of the "Blitz," saw the indomitable Churchill move from one bombed area to another, spreading courage and determination amid the ruins.

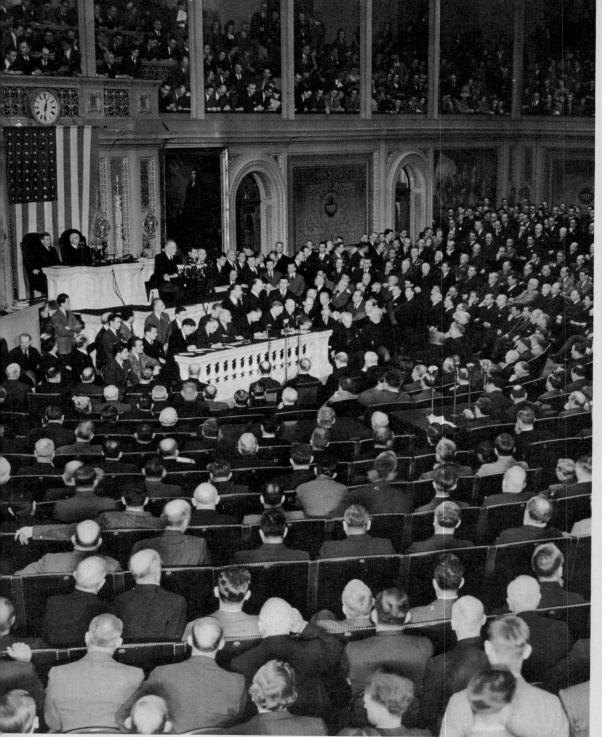

On December 7, 1941, history caught up with the United States. Next day, President Roosevelt asked a joint session of Congress to declare war against Japan (above).

Newsreelmen, recording the event from the House balcony, portrayed a solemn Congress unanimously resolved to wage total war until victory made peace-loving nations secure.

To prevent junction of Nazi and Jap in the Near East, Rommel's *Afrika Korps* had to be stopped. Montgomery turned the tide at El Alamein, routed the Germans in a four-month campaign. This shot is from films made by 26 British cameramen (of whom four were killed, seven wounded, eight captured), shown under the title *Desert Victory*.

Russia, too, threw back the Nazis in 1942. Here Red Army troops march through shattered Stalingrad, where mighty forces battled for 162 bloody days. Soviet photographers stayed so close to the lines that 13 were killed in action. Their work reached America in newsreels and in a documentary, *The City That Stopped Hitler—Heroic Stalingrad*.

Battle pictures from Tarawa (November, 1943) showed American movie-goers our own troops fighting to the death with the Japanese. Nothing like this had ever hit our public screens—the Naval bombardment of the tiny Pacific island, the incredible counter-lash of enemy fire as the Marines went in, the inch-by-inch advance past Japanese

block houses, trenches, gun emplacements, the Stars and Stripes finally fluttering over the blood-soaked atoll. The pictures, made on 16-mm. kodachrome, were rushed to the U. S. by plane. Black and white prints were used in the newsreels. An 18-minute Technicolor subject, *With the Marines at Tarawa*, was released nationally to 12,738 theaters.

This war's most imposing action—the Allied invasion of France in June, 1944—was also a photographer's field day. Newsreel cameramen went in with the combined forces on D-Day, covered the bitterly contested period from the first landings to the securing of beachheads and the unloading of supplies in huge quantities (above). Newsreel foot-

age, rushed to Great Britain to be cleared by the Allied Supreme Headquarters, reached the United States within 60 hours. It gave American audiences perhaps their proudest sight of the war. Hitler had hoped to save Germany by holding the Allies at the Atlantic coast; here was visual proof that his hope—like Hitler himself—was doomed.

CHAPTER III

TRAINING FILMS

Sheepish soldiers aimed wooden guns; trucks carrying signs reading "tank" rumbled across pastures; bivouacs were guarded by "artillery" made of logs—the Army of the United States was on maneuvers 18 months before Pearl Harbor.

The weapons of war were just beginning to trickle from factories. Before they finally came in a flood, special motion pictures, called training films, in many cases had taught our soldiers how to use them. For example, troops would be shown film describing the parts of a Garand rifle and proper methods of operating it. When Garands actually arrived in camp the soldiers were soon handling them like veterans.

In North Africa, in 1943, retreating Germans left behind a number of 88-mm. field guns. Our men could have used additional artillery, but few knew how to operate the enemy equipment. Training films showing them how were made on the spot and sped from company to company. In a matter of days, American artillerymen were blasting the Nazis with their own weapons.

At Aberdeen, Md., 30 soldiers sat through a film explaining the internal combustion engine. None had had previous instruction in the subject. But, given the test which winds up a lecture course on this engine, 27 of the 30 passed.

Such are the uses of training pictures in World War II—in which courage and skill in battle must be backed by mechanical equipment and the specialized knowledge needed to operate it. By standardizing teaching methods; by focusing attention on a screen instead of spreading it over blackboard, instructor and textbooks; by slow motion—revealing action too fast for the unaided eye—these films, it is estimated, have sped up the training of servicemen by as much as 40 per cent.

And the process has been painless. Plot, sound, music, color—long used to heighten the appeal of commercial motion pictures—have been combined to make training films a "show" to be enjoyed rather than instruction to be endured.

The teaching of soldiers through motion pictures dates back to the closing months of the last war, when 63 reels were produced under contract for the Army. Not sure then that such films were either necessary or effective, the Army did not start making its own training pictures for another decade. As recently as 1938 its training film staff consisted of three enlisted men, an officer and a civilian. Less than 20 films a year were made, while independent producers turned out as many more for the Navy, which has never made its own. Six years later, 20 training films were being made by and for the services every week.

In 1930, the non-profit Research Council of the Academy of Motion Picture Arts and Sciences had begun to train Army Signal Corps officers in motion picture production. By 1940, many of the senior officers in the Army training film program had learned the subject in Hollywood at Council expense. When the Draft Act was passed, and the military services quickly expanded, the Council also arranged for commercial studios to produce pictures needed to supplement the Army's own program. Hollywood's major studios made them at, or below, cost.

Five months after Pearl Harbor, the Army Pictorial Service (a branch of the Signal Corps) took over the former Paramount Pictures studio in Long Island City, N. Y., a modern, block-square plant with sound stages, workshops and technical facilities. By 1944, Colonel E. L. Munson, Jr., Chief of the Army Pictorial Service, had more men under his command than had been in the entire Signal Corps six years before. About 1,300 training films were made by the Army from Pearl Harbor to the end of 1944.

The range and variety of training films are astonishing. In the Army, the films accompany a man through every step of his progress: induction, orientation, training, off-duty activities, demobilization, and even preparation for his post-war life.

His screen education starts with essential preliminary information—*The Articles of War, Sex Hygiene, Military Courtesy.* Next he sees orientation films, such as the *Why We Fight* series (sample titles: *Prelude to War, The Nazis Strike, Battle of China*). Other pictures help condition him for battle. These may be as simple as *Keep It Clean* (how and why to take care of a gun), as moving as *Baptism of Fire.*

The latter shows a soldier going into battle for the first time. A voice interprets his thoughts, admits what his face shows—that he is afraid. The voice reassures him, explains that fear is natural, that it helps him protect his life, that if he weren't afraid he wouldn't be normal—and a good soldier. The soldier-actor in *Baptism of Fire* sees comrades killed or wounded. He is sickened and shocked by the sights and sounds of war. The voice analyzes these emotions, teaches

him—and through him the soldier audience —to overcome them and go on fighting. "Worth ten divisions," said one general staff officer of this training film.

When the soldier begins training in specific military operations, he is aided by "nuts and bolts" films, the backbone of the training program. These specialize in mechanical problems—how to build a bridge, how to dismantle a half-track, how to fight hand-to-hand. They often utilize combat footage to drive points home.

Other pictures, not meant strictly for training, deal with information and morale. An example is the bi-weekly *Army-Navy Screen Magazine,* shown to fighting men all over the world. Content ranges from pictures of the home front to eyewitness reports of combat. Every other issue presents *Snafu,* a cartoon character who points a moral by his comic boneheadedness. (In one film, Snafu goes to bed leaving a hole in his mosquito netting. The mosquitoes organize an army, attack Snafu, and give him malaria. The mosquito army, its mission completed, stages a review and awards decorations to the heroes of the assault.)

There are also combat bulletins, issued weekly, to show our troops how the war is being fought on all fronts. These are packed with subject matter to keep the soldier up to date about his own operations and those of troops in other parts of the world.

Finally, the soldier about to be discharged sees films designed to aid his return to civilian life (sample titles: *Opportunity Knocks Again, Your New Job*). If he is overseas when the shooting stops, subject to a long wait before shipping home, he can see films instructing him in a variety of civilian subjects, ranging all the way from auto mechanics to civics.

Because of the expense that would be involved in overlapping, and because of the shortage of raw film, the Army and Navy do not make training films on the same subjects. Each uses the films of the other.

The training film program helps to explain why Colonel Munson says that "the production of informational and combat films constitutes one of the most important developments of the war."

THIS FILM IS RESTRICTED   **THIS FILM IS CONFIDENTIAL**   **SECRET**

One of the three key phrases (above) introduces every training film produced by the Army. Only unclassified (i.e., non-confidential) pictures are made by outside studios.

Army recruits begin the transition from civilian to military life by watching *The Articles of War*, a movie setting forth their rights and obligations. This information formerly had to be read to soldiers every six months, a long, tiresome chore. The film is still dull by comparison with others but it can be run off in 47 minutes.

Servicemen see orientation films, such as *The Battle of China,* from the *Why We Fight* series. Purpose of this series is to give soldiers the background of World War II, show events leading up to our participation, reasons why our way of life is at stake. Avoiding propaganda, the series uses only combat footage, documentaries, other factual film.

A typical Navy training film—describing underwater techniques for student divers—is here shown in the making. The diver is a Navy man; the cameramen are civilians employed by the company that produced the picture under contract. This film was shot at Silver Springs, Fla., background of many peacetime Hollywood shorts on "aquabatics."

This face-to-face meeting with the business end of a coast-defense gun is typical of other Navy training films. For the Army, the Signal Corps has made training pictures covering 11 different kinds of heavy weapons. For each type of gun there is usually a film on servicing, one on drill, one on operation, one on placement, one on handling.

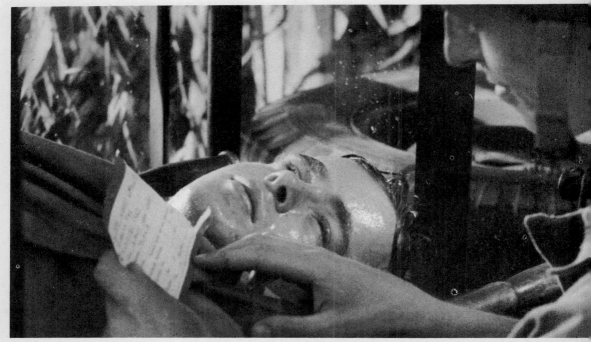

To aid and protect our wounded, photographers and technicians of the armed services have made pictures of all kinds. The first were simple, showing corpsmen how to use first-aid kits. Later they progressed through first aid in the snow to care of wounded in the tropics (above), the use of sulfa drugs, treatment of psychoneurosis.

Over a dozen films have been produced by the Army Air Forces to teach glider pilots to bring airborne troops down safely despite landing obstacles. Men who saw these, and other related training pictures later piloted the "50-mile glider train" which took off from England on D-day to spearhead our successful invasion of German-held Europe.

Army engineers prove their skill in the film *Clearing of Enemy Mine Fields*. Pictures on this subject were made under fire in Tunisia when our troops first encountered mines sown by the retreating Germans. The films, developed in an old Roman bathtub in a nearby Tunisian villa, were shown to soldiers entering the area, saved untold lives.

Facial camouflage, introduced in this war by the Japanese, is demonstrated in the Marine Corps film *Notes on Jungle Warfare*. Army Pictorial Service releases also discuss camouflage. They point out, for example, that planes at great heights can spot vehicle tracks and loose earth, and show how to cover tracks, dig foxholes that won't show.

CASTAWAY

Produced for the
BUREAU OF AERONAUTICS

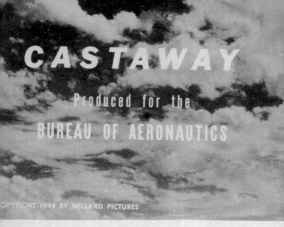

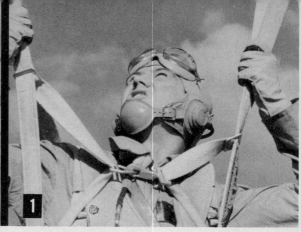

Here are scenes from a training film, with captions adapted from the sound track.

Well, here you are. The Jap got you; it couldn't be helped. Next stop: the water.

Get rid of that 'chute. When you hit the water you've got to get clear in a hurry.

Right. You're clear . . . Since the Nips aren't strafing you, inflate your boat.

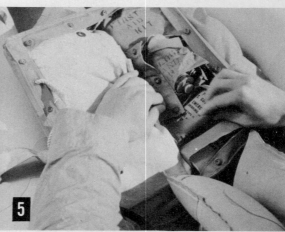

But now you stop to think. You're in a spot, Skipper, all alone with a whole ocean.

Still, it could be worse. You've got enough stuff in your boat to get you back.

6

So figure where you dunked, where you want to head, and get ready to go.

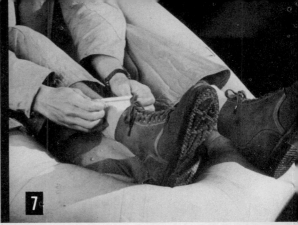

7

But first, watch that sun. Roll up your socks; don't let any part of you . . .

8

. . . get exposed. You've got to slap that ointment on right away.

9

Then you just shove off. It'll be slow going but paddle gloves will get you there.

10

A plane? It's one of ours. But it misses you in this bad weather. Tough luck, Skipper.

11

Now it's raining. You wash the salt crust off your face and drink fresh water.

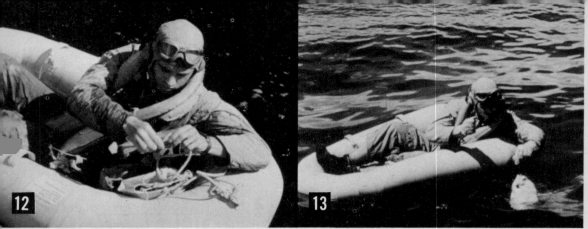

<table>
<tr><td>

12 You open your fishing kit. It's got everything in it you need . . .

</td><td>

13 . . . to catch your breakfast. You'll get ten ounces of juice out of that fish.

</td></tr>
</table>

14 Keep checking your map. You figure that land shouldn't be far away.

15 Yes, the map was right. It's an island. But it's solid and dry.

16 Sure looks empty. But don't stand there. Find water, and get out of that sun.

17 Remember what it said in the book about pig weed? It quenches thirst.

You're feeling better, now that you've made camp like a veteran.

Your next goal is more food. You're not too weak to go up for a coconut.

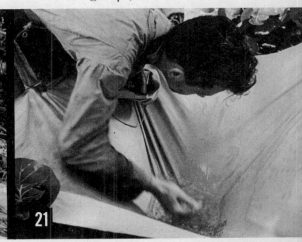

Crack it on a sharp stick. Coconuts and fish will keep you alive indefinitely.

Now you're on the beam. Even doped out a way to catch water in your boat cover.

Yes, you're all right. Just lonely. But the Navy hasn't forgotten you. And now . . .

. . . here's rescue. You've come through. Skipper, the Navy's proud of you!

51

One of the most colorful of the training film programs is that designed for Army paratroopers. Before the first combat jumps, films were made to cover all phases from packing the chute to killing or capturing the enemy. The airborne soldier is also conditioned psychologically for the circumstances he must face. Since he often fights behind

enemy lines, films teach him to become expert in demolition of power houses, railroads, bridges. He also sees films which give him a strong esprit de corps—such as *These Are the Paratroopers*. To insure its accuracy, the Army assigned a former Hollywood scenario writer to paratrooper school, where he learned to jump, then wrote the script.

Films like *Kill or Be Killed* (shots from it on this page and the next), seen before embarkation, tell the soldier he must be hard, like the cold-eyed character shown above.

1

In battle it's a free-for-all. *Kill or Be Killed* tells the soldier how to survive.

2

The Jap is the world's dirtiest fighter. Learn how to beat him at his own game.

3

The Nazi is trained to kill you first. If you run out of bullets, club him to death.

4

Use fists, feet, anything. The enemy won't give you a break. Never give him one.

5

Is he dead or faking? Got a knife? Make sure. Never forget that it's your life or his.

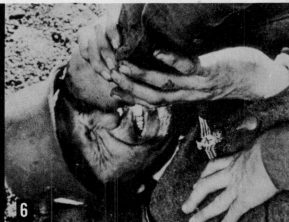

6

Jungle law is the law of the battlefield. Gouging and maiming make up the rules.

55

Here is Snafu, a favorite of servicemen, in a typical episode, titled *Booby Traps*.

Snafu is on the enemy's trail in the desert, where booby traps and boobs abound.

See? Pull the shower cord and BOOM! But Snafu isn't fooled. Not clever Snafu.

On to an oasis and a harem. What red-blooded soldier wouldn't tarry here?

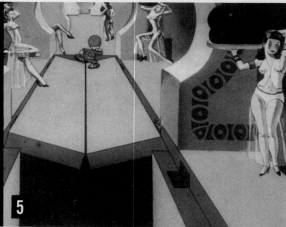

Oh-oh! Looks like the entrance to this harem was designed to snare 'em.

Snafu may yawn as he strolls carelessly along — but the floor yawns wider.

Safe so far, anyway. Gosh, what a spot!
(Our hero doesn't know they're dummies.)

Shall we smoke? It's TNT, but—oh, he's
burnt his finger. Now he doesn't want to.

Maybe a little music? And by the way,
what was all that talk about booby traps?

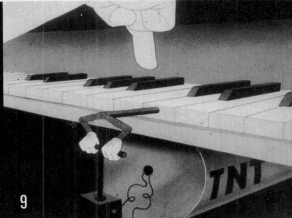

Well, Snafu, you're just about to find
out. Go ahead. Just hit that key . . .

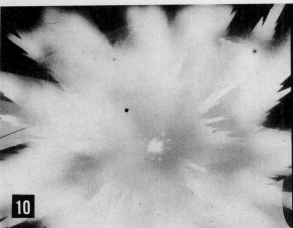

. . . and off we go, into the wide blue
yonder. That's Private Snafu all over!

So we've had fun, learned something too.
And so much for Snafu—till next time.

CHAPTER IV

COSTUMES BY UNCLE SAM

Time was when the most heroic hero in the world was the cinema variety. Back in the '30s, male leads often played characters whose daring was exceeded only by their indestructibility. The outbreak of war merely gave them a new melodramatic backdrop. Cast as Commandos, Flying Tigers, French underground fighters, they still won out no matter what the odds. Movie-going millions loved it.

Passage of the Draft Act in 1940, however, put cinematic heroes in a different light; Pearl Harbor turned the light to a glare. Here, the public suddenly realized, were healthy young Americans being paid whopping salaries to wipe out enemy battalions on the screen while other obscure young men all over the world were facing the real thing. Was that right? Deep down in public consciousness may have lurked a half-formed suspicion that the quickest way to win the war would be to give Jimmy Cagney a sawed-off shotgun, Errol Flynn a rapier, Wayne Morris a pair of boxing gloves, and Gary Cooper a squirrel rifle. Why, then, didn't Hollywood heroes enlist to a man? It was hard to credit the pedestrian fact that some were simply too old.

Two months after Pearl Harbor, Selective Service announced that film production was being classified as an essential industry. Britain, earlier in the war, had tried closing movie houses, but had reopened them quickly because of the morale value of screen entertainment. Our Government also wanted movies to continue; servicemen would need them even more than civilians.

But the Selective Service classification stirred the wrath of the Screen Actors' Guild, representing nearly 10,000 actors and actresses. The Guild was concerned lest the public howl "Preferential treatment!" It issued a statement that it did not agree with the classification. It declared that motion picture people should meet the same draft requirements as anyone else.

As it turned out, the Guild was over-anxious. Actors were treated like other draftable males, and so were the thousands of less well-known men in the industry's studios, offices and theaters. Some enlisted before the United States entered the war. Some went into uniform as their order numbers came up. And more kept going. By the end of 1944, more than 1,500 Guild members—including 49 stars and leading men—had entered the armed forces.

The services had also claimed 48 executives and producers, 132 members of the Screen Directors' Guild, 230 members of the Screen Writers' Guild, 40 cameramen, 75 electricians and sound technicians, 453 film technicians, 80 machinists, 2,000 musicians—nearly 40,000 of the 240,000 persons manufacturing, distributing, and exhibiting motion pictures.

An acute manpower shortage resulted, one that hit the industry hardest where it hurt most—on the screen. Movie-goers, deploring absence of their favorites, nevertheless demanded the kind of pictures to which those stars had accustomed them. One result was a mighty effort by the studios at wartime substitutions.

To fill dashing roles, aging actors were made to appear ten years younger, 20 pounds lighter, two inches taller and superhumanly braver than they were. Beardless youths, 4-F's, and actors discharged from the services came into demand; jealous studios even pooled their male talent. Wherever possible, stories were written to star women or children. And the show went on.

Meanwhile the industry had a direct role in the larger show going on outside its own bailiwick. Stars are always news; the first actor to enlist (David Niven; see page 61) touched off a press barrage that thunders again whenever a "big name" enters the Army. Ushers, studio guards, prop men, stand-ins and valets, however, cashed their last civilian paychecks and put on khaki or navy blue without any fanfare whatever.

Often the specialized background of the industry's workers has been of particular use to the services. Movie theater projectionists from all over the country utilized their abilities as Army technicians or Navy electrician's mates. Special-effects men—those wizards of the movie lots who manage to make things look like what they aren't—took naturally to camouflage work. Some studio cameramen turned to training films and to combat photography.

Men who had been working as producers, directors or public-relations experts went into uniform and undertook similar jobs for military film units. Many former members of the industry are still working together in the armed services although they are now thousands of miles apart. Consider the chain of events in the making, processing, and distributing of film footage shot during the 76-hour battle of Tarawa:

The Marine combat-photography unit that took the Tarawa pictures was headed by Capt. Louis Hayward, former movie star. Hayward sent his films to Capt. Gene Markey, USNR, onetime producer and writer, who was in charge of the Navy's motion picture branch. Markey put the films in a common pool of combat footage which went to the Army Signal Corps Photographic Center at Long Island City, N. Y. Head of the Center was Col. Emanuel Cohen, onetime executive at the Paramount Studios in Hollywood.

From Cohen the Tarawa footage passed to Maj. Kenneth MacKenna, former director and writer, part of whose job was to turn out industrial service films. (These, made mainly from combat footage, are designed to boost war workers' morale by showing them how the equipment they produce is used in action.) MacKenna selected sequences from the film, spliced them together and packed the finished product in cans. The cans went to Maj. Monroe Greenthal, formerly publicity head of United Artists, and Arthur Mayer, operator of New York's Rialto Theater, serving without pay as a civilian in the Army's Industrial Services Division. They distributed the picture to war plants and labor organizations.

Such is one aspect of filmdom at war. There are others:

Robert Montgomery, suave drawing-room comedian, having two destroyers shot from under him in the South Pacific . . . Clark Gable, screen idol, winning the Air Medal for bomber missions over German-held territory . . . Gene Autry, crooning cowboy, refused by the Air Forces because of age, taking flying lessons and getting into the Air Transport Command . . . Jackie Coogan, the "Kid" grown up, piloting the first glider landing behind Japanese lines in Burma . . . Douglas Fairbanks, Jr., urbane son of a famous father, winning the Silver Star for service at Salerno.

In this war, plenty of Hollywood actors have exchanged screen heroism for the real thing. But both actors and non-actors in the motion picture industry, both the "big names" who are always in the headlines and the multitude of "little fellows" who never make them, deserve credit for a military job well and faithfully done.

At an airfield in England, Clark Gable flashes his famous smile in conversation with Flying Fortress crew members. In 1942, Gable enlisted as a private in the Air Forces, trained in Miami, won a commission, rose to the rank of major, handled both camera and machine gun on missions over Europe before being put on the inactive list in 1944.

First Hollywood star to enter World War II, David Niven (center) returned to his native England in October, 1939, was commissioned a lieutenant in the British Army. (Here, with a British general, he inspects an army vehicle.) He went through the Dunkirk debacle, saw action with Commandos. In 1943, he became a lieutenant colonel.

While he was in England with the 8th Army Air Force, Col. William Wyler (left, chatting with Lt. Terrence Rattigan, British playwright) heard he had won an Academy Award for expert direction of *Mrs. Miniver*. He headed the film unit that made the breath-taking Technicolor feature picture of aerial operations, *The Memphis Belle*.

A veteran of the last war, producer-director Frank Capra (right) served in this one as a colonel in the Signal Corps. Entering the Army shortly after Pearl Harbor, he was assigned to Washington, produced the *Why We Fight* series of orientation films, later saw action in three combat theaters, won the Legion of Merit for his Army film work.

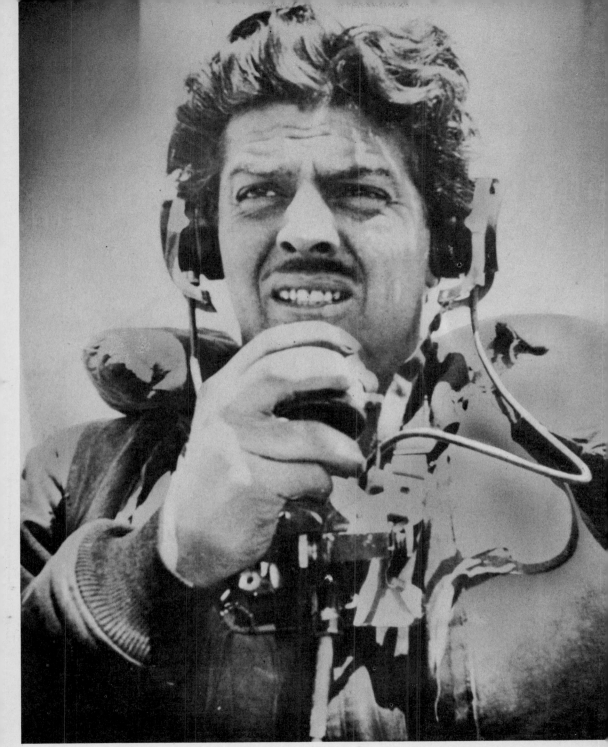

Victor Mature, handsome actor, enlisted in the Coast Guard Reserve (Temporary Class) in 1942. Honorably discharged, he re-enlisted in the regular Coast Guard next day, did 11 months of convoy duty in the North Atlantic, rose to the rating of chief boat-swain's mate, then toured America in the Spar's recruiting show, *Tars and Spars*.

Robert Montgomery, in 1940 a volunteer ambulance driver in France with the American Field Service, won a Navy commission, rose to the rank of lieutenant commander, saw action in the Atlantic, Pacific, Mediterranean. After six months at Guadalcanal, he fought in the Kula Gulf battle, commanded a destroyer during the invasion of France.

With three other Navy pilots, Wayne Morris (second from left) poses for a picture aboard their carrier after a strike against Formosa in 1944. Morris entered the Naval Reserve in 1942, was commissioned a lieutenant, won the Distinguished Flying Cross in 1944 for destroying seven Japanese planes, six on the ground and one in the air.

Tyrone Power enlisted in the Marines in 1942, won a commission and his wings as a pilot, was promoted to a first lieutenancy, is now on active service overseas.

A movie career died aborning in 1941 when Stirling Hayden joined the Merchant Marine. In 1942 he entered the Marines. He's shown here at boot camp.

In uniform before Pearl Harbor, Jackie Coogan transferred to the Air Forces, won the Air Medal as a glider pilot in Burma, where he got this Japanese flag.

Lew Ayres made news in 1942 when he was sent to a conscientious objectors' camp. Later he served honorably in the Army Medical Corps in the Philippines.

Enlisting in the Navy as an apprentice seaman in 1942, Henry Fonda saw active duty, worked his way up to the rank of lieutenant on staff duty, Air Combat.

Gene Raymond (pictured during a brief leave) received an Air Forces commission in 1942, served with the 8th AAF in England, returned to instruct pilots.

This agile young man is Pfc. Sabu Dastigar of the AAF, swinging through an obstacle course during training at Greensboro, N. C. Known to audiences merely as Sabu, the Indian-born star of *Elephant Boy* and other pictures was inducted (into the Army) in 1943. Soon afterward he became a U. S. citizen; later he was sent to the South Pacific.

British-born Louis Hayward (now a U. S. citizen) chose the non-glamorous job of combat photographer when he joined the Marines in 1941. As a captain, he headed the crack combat film unit at Tarawa, where he won the Bronze Star. This picture shows him after the fighting ended there. In 1944 he was given an honorable discharge.

Visiting a U. S. Navy vessel, King George of England shakes hands with a distinguished example of filmdom at war: Lt. Douglas Fairbanks, Jr. Commissioned before Pearl Harbor, Fairbanks was stationed in Washington and London, saw convoy duty in the North Atlantic, participated in the invasion of Sicily and the capture of Elba.

Part 2: JIMMY STEWART

On March 22, 1941, movie fans learned from their newspapers that filmdom—anticipating Pearl Harbor by nine months—had gone to war in the person of tall, dark-haired, wryly romantic James Stewart.

Stewart can be said to typify the thousands the industry has sent into uniform. He can be singled out for special mention because he was among the first to go and because he has been a singularly good soldier.

What few of his admirers knew is that the Stewart men of Indiana, Pa. (population 10,000), have a habit of getting into uniform whenever there's a war on.

James Maitland Stewart, founder and owner of the town's only hardware store, wore the blue during the Civil War, then returned to his place behind the counter. His son, Alexander, walked out of a Princeton classroom one day and went off to fight Spain. Like his father, he came back to Indiana to live out his life, but some years later found himself a captain in France, battling Germans. That war over, he finally settled down with the hardware store, his wife and his children: Mary, Virginia and Jimmy (born May 20, 1909).

It is possible that the present James Maitland Stewart was thinking of his fighting forebears when, in February, 1941, he ambled into a Los Angeles recruiting station and applied for the Army Air Corps. It is more likely that he was concerned with the excitement of flying: he owned his own monoplane, had logged 400 hours in the air. In any case, the Army turned him down. He weighed only 147 pounds—ten pounds too light for his gangling six feet four.

Stewart embarked on a diet of candy, beer and bananas. In one uncomfortable month he brought his displacement up to standard. Before he could enlist, however, his draft number came up. "First lottery I ever won," he drawled, and boarded a streetcar to the induction center.

Without fanfare, as quietly as his grandfather and father had left Indiana, Jimmy left Hollywood. Some people were surprised at that—but the folks back home would have been surprised at anything else.

For Jimmy Stewart, in or out of uniform, has clung to the spirit of his small-town American background. He grew up like millions of other boys—went to public school, dropped a hook in the creek of a summer, joined the Boy Scouts, fell in love and out again. The one thing that distinguished him was his accordion. His father had given it to Virginia, but it was too heavy for her. Jim annexed it, learned to play it with the help of the local Italian barber. The accordion went with him in 1924 to Mercersburg Academy, and in 1928 to Princeton.

At college Stewart made high marks in architecture, his planned career. On the side he joined the Princeton Triangle Club, dramatic group which puts on a musical show each winter in major Eastern and Midwestern cities. Touring with his accordion, he learned to like the stage. After graduation, he abandoned architecture to play and sing in a small night club run in connection with a summer theater on Cape Cod.

That fall, now definitely stage-struck, he went to New York. For a couple of years he hung around Broadway playing bit parts, then won the lead in *Yellow Jack*. Play and actor both clicked. Followed a screen test, a Hollywood contract, small roles in a few pictures, sudden success opposite Margaret Sullavan in *Next Time We Love*, then five years of stardom, spotlights, ever larger paychecks, fan clubs, world popularity.

Through all this the Stewart head remained well-balanced. A bachelor, he lived in a Los Angeles suburb, where he kept open house for friends. Come December, he liked to get back to Indiana and have Christmas dinner with the family. His lack of affectation, his warm understanding of other people's problems made him a favorite with his studio co-workers.

Yet James Stewart, $1,500-a-week movie star, knew he would have trouble winning acceptance from other servicemen as Pvt. Jim Stewart, A.U.S. When he began his training at Fort MacArthur, Cal., he was almost sure he was off on the wrong foot.

"I was just as much a problem to the Army when I first arrived as the Army was to me," he says. "The other recruits shied away from me a bit. That was natural."

But the tension was broken the next morning, when his sergeant made Stewart step up for his mail letter by letter. By the time the whole batch was delivered, the rest of the company was not only amused but friendly. In Stewart's words: "You can't stand off from a guy you've got on the pan." Thereafter he made his way as a soldier on his merits, not on his box-office draw.

He was a typical raw recruit. Fast dressing, after an early rising, was difficult for "a morning piddler by nature and long habit." Drill was fraught with menace for legs the length of his. And drill-trouble persisted; once, as a corporal, Stewart, taking a detail of 12 men to the hospital, marched them clear into some barracks by mistake. Like other soldiers, too, he did his share of griping. But he learned to like the Army, and he plugged hard at his job.

In due time he mastered the ground routine, was transferred to pilot training and, nine months after induction, won his wings and a commission as a second lieutenant.

Following further training, Stewart served as a flying instructor at fields in California, New Mexico and Idaho. Then, in August, 1943, he joined a Liberator bomber group at Sioux City, Iowa, as squadron commander. Four months later the group, assigned to the Eighth Army Air Force (strategic bombing), flew the Atlantic to England. Stewart now held the rank of captain.

Second motion picture star to be sent to the European Theater (after Clark Gable), he was the first to do active combat flying there. That made him news in Great Britain, where his fans wanted to hear what he had to say about things. But he made himself clear at once.

"I don't mean to be temperamental about this publicity stuff," he told a magazine correspondent. "If there's anything I can tell you about the job we're doing, I'll be glad to. . . . Right now that's all I have time to think about."

As squadron commander, Stewart was responsible for ten planes and 100 men. Within a month after his group reached England, he piloted his bomber (which has since been named *Nine Yanks and a Jerk*) on its first raid. Target: Bremen.

Stewart soon proved himself a capable flight officer, unruffled and determined under fire. In January, 1944, he was made a major—a rank he had previously refused to accept until, as he said, "my junior officers get promoted from lieutenants." A month later he had charge of 15 Liberators and the 150 men who took them into combat.

He was also doing excellent executive work on the ground. When the commander of a certain Liberator base wanted the best operations chief he could find, he chose Jimmy Stewart. In two months the base led its division in bombing efficiency. That helped win Stewart an appointment as combat-wing chief of staff to Brig. Gen. Edward Timberlake; by then (July, 1944) he had led his outfit on 14 missions over enemy territory in Europe.

Criticism of a celebrity who scales the military ladder rapidly is to be expected. Once Stewart got it from some visitors to his base. But his men told them off. They shared his pride when he won the Air Medal with Oak Leaf Cluster and, later, the Distinguished Flying Cross. They approved when he was made a lieutenant colonel.

Late in 1944 they heard even better news: Jim Stewart was now a colonel.

Stewart himself has consistently underplayed his accomplishments, given major credit to his men. Though pleasant and friendly, he has concentrated on work and sometimes puzzled associates by his reticence. Says one: "He is plenty okay, but for a movie actor he is certainly publicity-shy. All he wants is to be left alone."

From the start, James Stewart decided to divorce himself from his cinematic name and fame, and in this he succeeded. He has frequently joked, as soldiers will, about his hometown: "It's really something. It's been sweating it out to be a real city for a long time." But on the official record that hometown is Indiana, Pa., not Hollywood.

When Stewart received the Distinguished Flying Cross, a photographer, aware of his dislike of personal publicity, hesitantly asked to film the ceremony. "I'll be proud to have the picture taken," Stewart said. They were proud of that picture in Hollywood, too. And in Indiana, Pa.

Here is James Stewart of Hollywood before the war—with Ginger Rogers on the set of *Vivacious Lady* (1938). His first hit, *Next Time We Love*, was made in 1936. Other successes included: *You Can't Take It with You* (1938), *Made for Each Other* (1939), *Destry Rides Again* (1939), *The Mortal Storm* (1940), *Come Live with Me* (1941).

And here is Lieutenant Stewart of the Army Air Forces as he looked in 1942 after a year and a half of military service. Gone are the klieg lights and make-up of the movie lot; in their place, there appear fierce sunlight of the upper air and a face that bespeaks a fighting man's determination. When Jimmy Stewart went to war, he went the whole way.

A quarter-century ago the Stewart family of Indiana, Pa., assembled on the front porch for this picture. Left to right: Mrs. Stewart, Mary, Mr. Stewart, Virginia, and Jimmy.

Film celebrity Stewart willingly gave fans his autograph. But in the Army he sought obscurity, hoped people would think of him only as a soldier, not as a star in uniform.

Perhaps the best-remembered scene from Stewart's movie career is the climactic Senate speech he made in *Mr. Smith Goes to Washington*. This 1939 picture, in which he co-starred with Jean Arthur, gave him the sort of role that helps explain his wide popularity: that of an earnest, fumbling, humorous young man with shy, romantic appeal.

Stewart's interest in aviation dates back to boyhood and model-plane building. He had a private pilot's license a year before he entered the Army and he spent many an hour with the Stinson monoplane (above) he acquired in 1940. Even while shooting a picture, he found time to work out, with his mechanic, a new type of carburetor de-icer.

Of the 28 movies James Stewart made during his seven years in Hollywood, the biggest box-office smash was *The Philadelphia Story* (1940). This comedy of Main Line society was adapted from Philip Barry's stage play. Its success was partly attributable to Katharine Hepburn (above) and Cary Grant, to top direction and a bubbling love story.

His superb performance in *The Philadelphia Story* won Stewart filmdom's highest honor: an "Oscar," awarded to him as the year's best actor by the Motion Picture Academy of Arts and Sciences. His acceptance speech was the shortest on record: "Thanks." Here he beams over the bronze figure at Ginger Rogers, winning actress, and comedian Bob Hope.

A few days after the 1941 Academy Award dinner (top picture), civilian Stewart was sworn into the Army with 18 other inductees. About 100 loyal fans, mostly women, gathered to give him a send-off. His arrival at the draft board produced two characteristic lines: "Hullo"—and then, with a sleepy grin, "Uh, it's a little early in the morning."

This photograph commemorates the two months the ex-actor spent as a flying instructor at the United States Flying Training Command's Bombardier School (Albuquerque, N. M.). With five bombardiers-to-be, Lieutenant Stewart (third from left) poses in front of an advanced trainer before taking off on a high-altitude bombing run.

Under Army orders, Stewart revisited Hollywood for a brief period in 1941 to make the recruiting short, *Winning Your Wings* (credited by the Army with gaining thousands of Air Forces recruits). Here he attends a movie première with (left to right) his agent, Leland Hayward; Margaret Sullavan, Hayward's wife; screen actress Kay Aldrich.

The day the Allies invaded France, Stewart —as group operations officer of a Liberator base in England—distributed flight forms to bomber pilots for their missions in support of the amphibious forces. A lieutenant colonel at the time, Stewart had this responsible job because of his own combat record and long hours of excellent administrative work.

This is the kind of job the Air Forces called on Stewart and his men to do—a bombing attack on Brunswick, Germany. Targets: a tank factory, a Messerschmitt plant, an airfield (top of picture). In similar raids on Berlin, Frankfort, Kiel, Bremen and several other cities, Stewart did his bit to help cripple Adolf Hitler's industrial might.

And this is the reward for a bombing mission over Brunswick, carried out February 20, 1944, in the face of furious enemy fighter attack and antiaircraft fire: Lt. Col. R. D. Potts pins the Distinguished Flying Cross on Col. James Stewart, onetime screen star, here the proud living symbol of the entire motion picture industry's men in uniform.

CHAPTER V

FOXHOLE CIRCUIT

The soldiers sit in the dark of a jungle night, jammed together on makeshift benches, hot and sweaty and dirty and tired — waiting. Tropical insects dig at their faces and necks. There is a gust of warm rain, a growl of thunder. Somewhere a gun speaks. Still they wait, doggedly. For what?

Well, for one of the few breaks in war's monotony that can give men simultaneous laughter, refreshment and a momentary illusion of being home again. Not chow. Not payday. Not even mail call. Instead—

Light rises, uncertain (Army generators get shaky in jungle dampness), focuses on a rough board platform. Figures appear. The crowd's mutter is stilled.

An officer steps forward on the stage. "And now, fellows, direct from Hollywood and points west, the famous little lady you've all been waiting for, with her talented troupe of entertainers—"

Cheers, whistles; then expectant silence. The actress sings a song. She tells some jokes. Her accompanist plays his accordion. There's a short dramatic skit, maybe a well-remembered scene from one of her pictures. And, after each number, applause — loud, warm, unself-conscious.

Then encores. Wisecracks from the dark benches. Experienced answers from the platform (she's heard the wisecracks before). More encores — the songs men sing when they think of home. And then everybody singing together, forgetting tension, forgetting battles and killing, feeling like civilians having fun on Saturday night.

For the little time the show lasts, the men are taken straight to the familiar Main Street that is the goal of every fighting American far away from home.

Tomorrow night the entertainers will be elsewhere with their magic. But not soon will they be forgotten.

No one asks, or expects, dentists or draftsmen or district attorneys to go overseas in the middle of a war and sweat out arduous hours without pay; but everyone assumes that movie stars are only too glad to. Oddly, in most cases everyone is right.

Even before America entered the war, entertainment for troops in camp was recognized as vital to morale. Movies were one obvious answer (see Part 3 of this chapter), but more was needed. Why not live shows?

Why not? The United Service Organizations had the facilities, and in October, 1941, the branch known as USO Camp Shows was set up. Booking agents, producers, writers and music arrangers agreed to lend a hand. Entertainers of all kinds were approached—top stars (stage and radio as well as motion picture) to donate their services, lesser luminaries to be paid from funds contributed to the USO by the public.

Late in 1941 the first camp show, a variety bill, was presented at Fort Bragg, N. C. That fired the starting gun. As Pearl Harbor led to the mass movement of our fighting men all over their country and then the world, live entertainment followed. In three years following Pearl Harbor, some 3,500 performers made more than 35,000 personal appearances.

Four "circuits," dwarfing the most lavish operations of the old vaudeville days, were created. In the United States, at 600-odd Army posts and Naval stations with adequate theaters, the *Victory Circuit* put on full-sized revues, plays, concerts. Smaller troupes played the *Blue Circuit*—the 1,150-plus installations lacking first-rate theaters and other facilities. The *Hospital Circuit* furnished entertainment in wards and auditoriums of military hospitals.

And, overseas, stars and their supporting players began to appear on the *Foxhole Circuit*. By the end of 1944, fully 2,000 performers (about one in six was a "big name" working without compensation) had gone on USO tours outside the United States. Many had made two or three trips. The roster of traveling stars read like the Casting Directory of Hollywood—Joe E. Brown (see Part 2 of this chapter), Bob Hope, Jack Benny, Bing Crosby, Ann Sheridan, Paulette Goddard, Gary Cooper and so on.

Of all the USO Circuits, the *Foxhole* posed the biggest problems—transportation, itineraries, weather conditions, availability of talent. But difficulties were overcome. Eventually the Army Special Services Division — or the Bureau of Naval Personnel — could request entertainment in the same terse language used to order tanks or tins of C-ration, and be sure of having the request as quickly filled.

Suppose the Army wants five entertainers, including one Hollywood star and one musician, to play the Far East for six months. Camp Shows gets in touch with the minor performers and asks the Hollywood Victory Committee (established for just this sort of thing) to see what outstanding "names" can be recruited from motion pictures.

Within two weeks the troupe is picked, assembled in California (in New York for a European tour), told what is expected of it, given "shots" as protection against disease. Then it waits for marching orders.

Meanwhile the troupe's material (built around the star) is written, rehearsed, tried out. The Army may suggest changes or censor lines. But once the show is set, the traveling players rarely deviate from it. Nor, once under way, do they disobey Army orders. For the Army supplies their transportation, food and audiences.

It is the audiences that make the whole thing pay off. Otherwise, giving up hundreds or thousands of dollars a week to amuse people in far away places would hardly be popular, especially in view of the hardships involved. But GI Joe's enthusiasm makes it all worthwhile.

In this war, Hollywood players have given shows in jungles, deserts, tundras; on islands from Iceland to Australia; on beachheads, just behind the front lines; amid air raids, within range of enemy guns; in post theaters seating thousands and in wilderness outposts reachable only by mule-back, dog-sled, transport plane, or canoe.

Paulette Goddard, for example, flew the perilous "hump" over the Himalaya Mountains in an Army plane. She was the first woman civilian to take the risk. On her trip through the backlands of Southeast Asia she washed her face in leftover tea, brushed her teeth in grapefruit juice. She went to spots —and endured discomforts—that "even Joe E. Brown missed." But she loved it. The welcome she received wherever she went, from Americans cut off by time and distance from all the familiar things that spell home, was her compensation.

During the bloody 1942-43 campaign that freed North Africa from German domination, singer Ella Logan was giving a performance for several hundred men in an oversized Nissen hut. After two hours—during which she had been on the stage more than an hour answering endless pleas for popular songs—Miss Logan called out half-hopefully, "Fellows, am I keeping you from anything?"

The answer came quickly from a youngster seated well back in the audience. "Yeah," he assured her. "Suffering."

A top favorite with GI's the world over is Bob Hope, movie-radio gagman extraordinary. Here he is shown (right) with singer Frances Langford and guitarist Tony Romano before a delighted audience in Sicily, on the second of four overseas trips—which together covered more than 150,000 miles—in the two years ending September, 1944.

On Bougainville a soldier spotted Bob Hope and shouted, "Hey, fellas, here comes Trader Corn." Hope enjoys gags like that more than he does his own. Here at Pearl Harbor, the first stop on a 30,000-mile tour, Hope tries out a .50 cal. machine gun as Frances Langford looks on. He called the tour the Sarong Circuit and the Mosquito Network.

In the South Pacific (above), Bob Hope was mobbed by servicemen from Hawaii to Australia. At the end of 1944 he had given shows for 2,000,000 men overseas. Global entertainment may be accompanied by worse hazards than discomfort. In 1943 two members of a USO Camp Shows troupe were killed when their plane crashed at Lisbon.

First USO show to go outside the U. S. was "The Flying Showboat," which toured Caribbean bases by air in November, 1941. The troupe—Stan Laurel and Oliver Hardy (above), Jane Pickens, Ray Bolger, John Garfield, Mitzi Mayfair—suffered from heat, rain, insects, many shows on little sleep, but proved that soldiers love live entertainment.

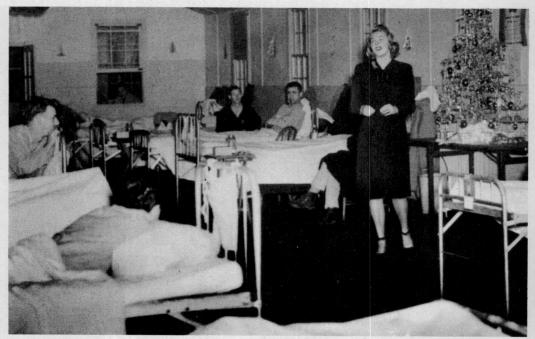

Actress Ingrid Bergman, in a midwinter (1943-44) tour of Alaska and the Aleutians by boat and plane, wore afternoon dresses instead of evening gowns, sang Swedish folk songs to hospitalized men (as she is doing above). Because she looks and acts like an idealized version of their own best girls, she is a great favorite among servicemen.

The Japs still held Kiska and Attu when Marjorie Reynolds, shown with two soldiers, visited the Alaskan Theater in the spring of 1943. She covered 7,000 miles in eight weeks with 55 pounds of luggage, endured fog, snow, bitter cold, symbolized the many unpublicized entertainers who are known to thousands of men in combat areas.

Four who made a smash hit in England, Ireland and North Africa in 1942-43 were Mitzi Mayfair, Kay Francis, Carole Landis (above, front center) and Martha Raye (behind Miss Landis). They traveled 37,-000 miles, were fired on over the Mediterranean, ate Army food, survived bombing. "They deserve medals," wrote Ernie Pyle.

John Garfield, who was one of the "Flying Showboat" group (p. 86), also trouped the Mediterranean early in 1944 with Jean Darling and Sheila Rogers (above), and Eddie Foy, Jr. They covered the "mud circuit" (Italian front-line areas and air bases), appeared within three miles of the lines at Cassino, once played for Yugoslav guerrillas.

This is Al Jolson, long-run comedian of screen, stage and radio, entertaining outside a hospital at Palermo, Sicily, in 1943, during his fourth volunteer overseas tour (others: Alaska, England, the Caribbean). On this trip he traveled 40,000 miles, spent 164 hours in the air, played about 120 shows, saw Italy's fleet surrender to the Allies.

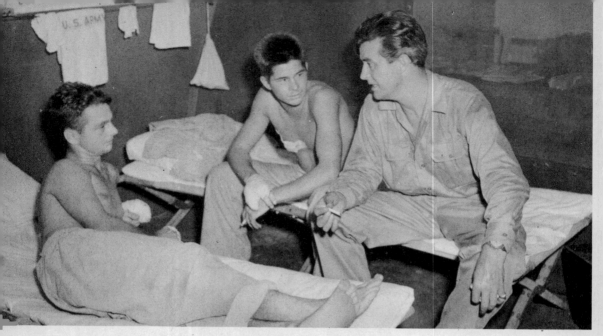

A ten-week South Pacific tour in 1944 took Ray Milland (right) and three girl entertainers to Australia, New Caledonia, the New Hebrides, the Solomons, the Russell Islands. They moved mainly by air, saw the worst kind of fighting conditions, experienced intense discomfort, came back filled with respect for our hard-working troops.

Comic dancer Ray Bolger and pianist-singer Little Jack Little (who mastered the accordion for the occasion) put in five solid months together around the South, Southwest and Central Pacific in 1943. They flew 27,000 miles, played to crowds of from 50 to 14,000, were out so long that finally the soldiers were teaching *them* the new songs.

This big-name troupe hit the Southwest Pacific late in 1943. Here, Gary Cooper stands by while Una Merkel speaks into the mike. Men everywhere asked Cooper for Lou Gehrig's "Farewell to Baseball." One night the lights failed in mid-show; at once 10,000-odd flashlights in the audience were focused on the stage. The show went on.

Early in 1944 Paulette Goddard became the first actress to visit the China-Burma-India Theater, found GI's as eager for her autograph as fans back home. She played every hospital and American base in the area (130 shows), once found herself five miles from the Japanese lines. With her were Keenan Wynn, William Gargan and Andy Arcari.

While his buddies await their turns, a Marine at a South Pacific base tries an impromptu dance step with USO entertainer Patti Thomas. This shot, showing one of the more active attacks on the problem of entertaining servicemen, was taken during a 1944 tour. On it were Bob Hope, Frances Langford (see p. 84), Jerry Colonna and others.

Another star-studded group in the South-west Pacific: (left to right) singer Martha Tilton, harmonica virtuoso Larry Adler, Carole Landis, Jack Benny, pianist June Brunner. Audience: a Papuan native. Occasion: a 30,000-mile, 140-show tour in 1944. Adler, Miss Landis and Benny had previously played Europe and North Africa.

Myitkyina, air base in Burma, was one stopping point for Ann Sheridan on her 8-week USO tour of the CBI Theater. Although the field hospital was miles from the unit Ann was entertaining, she insisted she be allowed to meet all the boys who had fought for Myitkyina. Above, she watches a card game among three hospitalized Marauders.

Before massed GI's in France, songstress Dinah Shore swings into a hit tune. This screen luminary and her troupe toured England and France for eight weeks in 1944. They gave 130 shows, often close behind the retreating Germans. When she and Bing Crosby sang a radio appeal to Germans to surrender, Nazis dubbed Bing "Der Bingle."

Midwinter, 1943-44, found Humphrey Bogart and his wife, Mayo Methot, playing in Italy, Sicily, North Africa and England. At Casablanca in Morocco (above), the fictional scene of his best-known screenplay, *Casablanca*, Bogart tried to satisfy numerous queries from servicemen by looking up "Rick's Café." Turned out he couldn't find it.

This "gag shot" records the August, 1944, crossing of two European tours: those of Fred Astaire (left) and Bing Crosby. Pretending to mistake Bing's crooning expression for one of pain, Fred offers an anesthetic. Lt. Ruby C. Wills, ANC, readies a giant hypodermic. Like most USO players, Fred and Bing returned eager to go back.

Part 2: ONE-MAN LAUGH WAVE

In sheer devotion to America's fighting men and to the job of making their grim lives more bearable, none of filmdom's traveling entertainers surpasses a middle-aged comedian whose principal comedy prop is an enormous mouth.

His name is Joe E. Brown. He was the first Hollywood star to tour Alaska and the Aleutians, first in Southwest Pacific combat waters, first in the China-Burma-India Theater. From March, 1942, to February, 1944, he covered more than 150,000 miles, paying all his own expenses except when traveling by Army plane.

His third overseas trip during that period rolled up 47,000 miles in just three months, delighted troops in Brazil, Nigeria, the Sudan, India, China, Burma, Iran, Iraq, Egypt, Tunisia, Algeria, Italy, Morocco. Only Bob Hope can lay claim to similar geographical coverage.

Around the world, in hundreds of bases, camps and outposts, men have vowed him a very funny fellow. To the connoisseur of comics, his routine may seem neither witty nor inventive. His jokes are unsophisticated, lily-pure (he never even mentions a woman); his delivery is far from subtle. Yet our servicemen love him.

They love him in part for his utter sincerity, his willingness to go anywhere under any conditions. "He came up here—*and he didn't have to!*" In the frozen desolation of Alaska they said that again and again.

His patter may be time-tried and familiar, but, being familiar, it draws a quick response. Brown has quipped about Brooklyn in the mucky, sweating jungles of the Pacific, in the searing oven of Iran, against a backdrop of enemy shellfire in Italy. And Brooklyn always gets laughs—half amused and probably half homesick.

Servicemen love him because he knows how to talk to young men. He discusses one of their pet subjects, sports, with the authority of one who used to play baseball professionally when theatrical engagements were slack. He gripes good-naturedly about GI equipment and food. "One reason I came out here was that I couldn't get any Spam at home." He knows how to kid the things that are close to the everyday existence of servicemen because he has lived with them, shared their tents, eaten their rations, been under fire and, with them, agonized for mail from home.

Between shows (he sometimes does ten a day) he tries to meet and talk to every serviceman in the vicinity. In one camp he signed his name 1,000 times in a day—"autographed my arm off," he wrote his wife gleefully. From China he summed up his work with deep satisfaction: "I don't think we missed more than 200 men."

When America entered this war, Joe E. Brown was nearing his 50th birthday, a married man with grown children. (Both sons and his ward, ex-football star Mike Frankovich, joined the Army Air Forces.) He had come up the hard way in show business, made 65 movies and plenty of money, become one of Southern California's solid citizens. Had he so desired, he might have sat back to watch the war from Beverly Hills.

But watching wasn't enough — especially after Brown received a letter from a soldier in Alaska saying the boys were lonesome for a familiar face. Brown understood that. At ten, he'd run away from home (Holgate, Ohio) to be an acrobat, bumped around for years playing cheap carnivals, tent shows, vaudeville circuits — on his own. He well knew what loneliness can mean.

Hence the instant decision: he and his big grin were heading north on a morale job. They went so fast that the Government telegram granting permission for the trip caught Brown when he was already in Alaska. In two months he gave 132 shows all over that territory and the Aleutians. Once he clowned for 600 men while 1,500 more waited for hours outside in 25-below-zero weather. Once his plane was lost in an Arctic storm; he heard later that men on the ground bet 30 to one it would never land safely. In the primitive village of Gambell — 298 Eskimos, five whites — the date of his visit was honored by a proclamation: "We, the council . . . say and make rule that every March 19 must be holiday called Mr. Joe E. Brown Day because he make happy this day . . ."

That was the first trip. A few months later the comedian's son, Capt. Don E. Brown, was killed in a bomber crash. Grief-stricken, Joe E. Brown signed up mentally for as many overseas trips as he could take—for the duration.

"When you have lost your own boy," he says in his book, *Your Kids and Mine,* "all other lads become your sons."

He started out again in January, 1943, for the South and Southwest Pacific. The tour lasted four months, took him to the most remote islands then in American hands. His smallest audience was two sick youngsters in a hospital tent; his largest, some 15,000 soldiers, sailors, Marines, and Seabees at a base in New Caledonia. In New Guinea he gave shows just six minutes' flying time from the Japs. On Canton Island one man had to miss the fun because he was up the island's only tree on lookout duty, so Brown climbed up beside him for a personal chat. Once he put on his act for four soldiers doing patrol duty on a lonely hill—later the hill was named after him. Countless uncharted Pacific Islands also bear his name. On Guadalcanal a road near Henderson Field is called "Rue de Joe E. Brown."

No other actor has had the advance publicity Brown got in the Pacific. During his tour his name became a password among Navy radio operators. Night after night, in the warming-up period before opening on code, they would flash the message: "Joe E. Brown is coming." "What! The big-mouthed fellow?" "That's the one."

In November, 1943, the tireless little comedian said good-bye to his wife and two daughters, set off a third time. With him, as military aide and pilot-if-necessary, went his "adopted son," Captain Frankovich; also pianist-composer Harry Barris. Before they got home they had put on more than 200 performances.

In India they gave shows in the big cities, then flew out to the frontiers. Of one strenuous day Brown wrote home: "The kids have gone nuts and have eaten up every try for a laugh. Day before yesterday we landed on an 800-foot strip in Piper Cub planes and did a show on the strip way up (3,000 feet) in the mountains . . . We then were driven 14 miles in 3 hours and 40 minutes to do another show. Our night show was done with three bulbs on the planks and the lights of two jeeps."

Brown flew with two bombing missions in China, one in Burma. From China he wrote: "We are now at the end of the line... We are the very first that have come in . . . These kids surely show their appreciation."

In Cairo he did a show with three kings in the audience—Peter of Yugoslavia, George of Greece, Farouk of Egypt. In Italy the Brown troupe put up for a while in a 2,600-room palace built in 1791, staged several shows with German planes overhead.

But it is not the adventures, the narrow escapes and odd stories he picks up that impress Brown most about his overseas entertaining. It is what one homely fellow with a gift for clowning can do for tired, high-strung men fighting a global war.

A doctor in the Pacific told him, "The only thing that can relax bodies as taut as these is a tub of hot water—or a good belly laugh. And we can't get the hot water."

More than once Brown has done his stuff while he was exhausted, hungry, even half sick. But he has always managed to evoke those belly laughs.

From India he wrote of a show at a hospital: "Gee, a cold chill went up and down my spine as those boys lay there and laughed. The reaction to that one show paid me for any and all discomforts of the trip."

Brown has received a variety of honors for his outstanding military trouping. The National Father's Day committee awarded him its Eisenhower Medal as "1944 Father to All Men Overseas."

He has had thousands of letters from parents whose boys overseas write them of his endless good humor and his personal interest in their welfare. Most of the parents want Brown to visit them. Right after his 1943-44 trip he accepted at least one such invitation from the parents of servicemen—to dinner at the White House.

But he is proudest of what Gen. Douglas MacArthur said when the comedian met him in Brisbane, Australia: "There isn't a man, in uniform or out, who has done more for our boys than you have, Mr. Joe E. Brown."

Alongside an American vessel berthed in a Pacific port, one of the Army's favorite pin-up boys creates a guffaw for the Navy. This is the Joe E. Brown our soldiers, sailors, Ma-rines, Coast Guardsmen know best: the brown hair brushed smoothly back, the blue eyes sparkling, the vast mouth split in an equally vast grin, the whole five-feet-seven

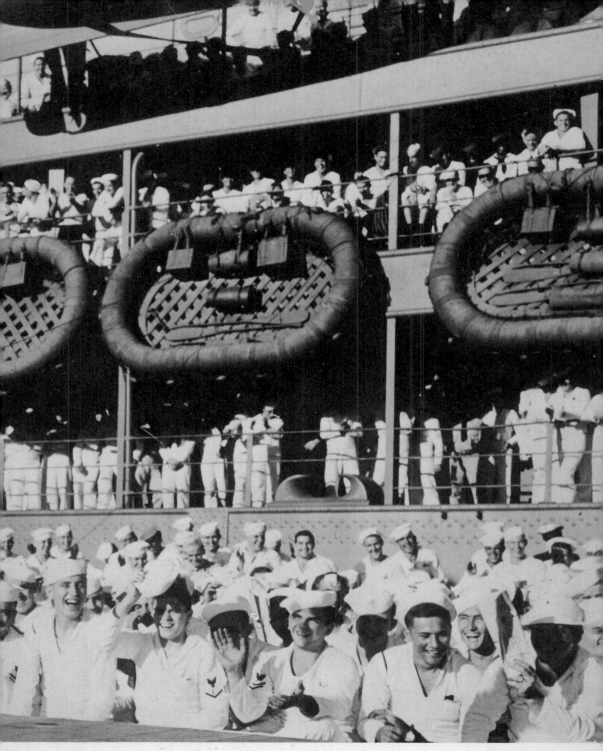

of him moving in exaggerated pantomime. When the body calms down, the mouth springs into action: "Anyone here from Brooklyn? . . . Oh, you don't want to admit it. Don't be afraid, you're among friends. Why, I once knew a swell guy from Brooklyn. . . . He was an MP." This is the Joe E. Brown heard—and adored—all around the world.

Brown has lifted the morale of men in uniform the world over. But his efforts have not been limited to fighting men. Here, on the Isle of Lei Lei, New Guinea, he meets the same warm welcome he gets from GI's. Brown has entertained civilian residents in China, the Fiji Islands, Arabia, New Zealand, Burma, Italy, Egypt and the Gold Coast.

The dignity of gold braid thaws before Brown's clowning—witness Adm. William Halsey (second from left) and Brig. Gen. Hubert Harmon (at his left) enjoying the enlisted men's delight at a Pacific base. Brown's book describes meetings with MacArthur, other top military men. His conclusion: "Generals are just like other people."

During a midday show in New Caledonia, the mobile Brown mouth co-operates in a burlesque of Hitler promising Germany the world. Jeep in background stands by to rush Brown to his next stand. Such fast travel over rough military highways results in gags like, "I sure enjoyed the ride here on your lovely road, men. Best road I ever tasted."

Brown is pictured talking to his elder son, Don, who is shown here as an air cadet, and to whom he was devoted. Capt. Don Brown crashed to his death on October 8, 1942.

Here is one way Brown expresses his feeling for American boys—by mingling with them as a friend, and not as a celebrity. The scene of this particular pool game: Sitka, Alaska.

Christmas in India was no day of rest for Brown. He saw the Taj Mahal, flew to New Delhi, toured a hospital, gave this outdoor show, had cocktails with 16 generals.

New Guinea: the comedian autographs bills for fellow Short Snorters. This club is open to those who have flown overseas; member must produce bill on demand or buy a drink.

For once Joe E. Brown fails to get a smile: the Chinese baby (wearing a tiger hat to ward off evil spirits) just won't play. The baby is highly unusual. From Chungking to Naples, from New Guinea to Nome, the comedian has been a one-man laugh wave. To literally millions of servicemen Joe typifies Hollywood's role in World War II.

Part 3: BEACHHEAD BIJOU

This war has scattered millions of American fighting men far across the face of the globe. Even in the most remote spots, however, they have taken regular "two-hour furloughs home" via American movies.

Ten days after the Allies launched their June, 1944, invasion of France, troops in Normandy were whistling appreciatively at Rita Hayworth in *Cover Girl*. Soldiers who led our advance into Germany saw a movie three days later on German soil. Shortly after General MacArthur's fighters went ashore on Leyte, in the Philippines, they were watching a double-feature program fresh from Hollywood.

Like live entertainment, movies relax and divert minds battered by combat or stagnant with boredom. But the importance of "two-hour furloughs" goes beyond that. To men overseas, they are a link with home second only to mail. And films have one great practical advantage over flesh-and-blood entertainers: they can be shipped in small cans anywhere supply lines are open.

The Army Pictorial Service, through its Overseas Motion Picture Service, began capitalizing on this advantage right after Pearl Harbor. For years the Army and Navy had rented standard 35-mm. prints and shown them in post theaters, aboard ships and at shore installations. The Navy still maintains standard projection equipment on its larger ships and at the end of 1944 there were more than a thousand War Department theaters for troops within the United States. In February, 1942, however, the motion picture industry offered to make 16-mm. prints of all Hollywood pictures available to all services, without charge, for showing in combat areas, hospitals and isolated outposts overseas.

From that time to the end of 1944, the OMPS shipped out more than 25,000 prints of feature films and newsreels, and more than 30,000 prints of short subjects. Three programs a week went from the main film exchange in New York (staffed by both Army and Navy men) to 21 overseas exchanges, thence to advanced areas. In a single day, more than 1,150,000 servicemen have attended more than 3,000 film showings. Audiences have included soldiers, sailors, marines, Coast Guardsmen, nurses, USO and Red Cross workers, Allied troops, friendly civilians, even small groups of enemy prisoners.

At the start there were too few Army and Navy projectors to go around, and distribution problems were numerous and complicated. But the serious obstacles were overcome. By January, 1943—when *Arsenic and Old Lace* had its world première overseas— many of our troops were seeing pictures that had not yet been released to civilian audiences back home.

Servicemen have honored their "movie houses" with names half-nostalgic, half-humorous—Radio City Music Hall, Loew's Bougainville, The Eyestrain. They have done their film-going under conditions that would baffle the hard-boiled theater managers of New York's fiercely competitive 42nd Street. They have sat in muddy jungle clearings, ice-covered Quonset huts, battered barns, open-air amphitheaters, on hillsides, beaches, on ship decks in the moonlight and jammed into reeking heat below decks while in enemy waters.

In Hawaii, the Navy started the "submarine circuit" to provide U-Boat crews with film fare to brighten their long cruises.

In the Aleutians, men packed a little mess hut and projected the pictures on a thin screen so that they could be viewed from both sides. In the Southwest Pacific, native islanders were thus watching a film "backward" when a local buck lost his temper at the villain and threw a coconut at him. It went through the parachute-silk screen, hit an officer watching on the other side, knocked him unconscious.

On the Anzio beachhead in Italy, there was a comedy on the screen when a stray German shell exploded nearby. A moment later—to the delight of the shell-conscious audience—a film character spoke the line, "What was that?"

Army Pictorial Service officers at overseas exchanges have instructions to deliver the newest films to the front lines. As one writer has put it, "The man who fires the first shot sees the first show." This is as it should be. But there are others to whom the morale value of movies is inestimable. These are the men at lonely outposts and isolated observation points—men as valuable in their way as combat troops, but faced with a different foe: boredom.

If these men think they are forgotten by the folks at home, they cease to be efficient cogs in our global military machine. To them, and to American war prisoners (who receive the gift films through the Y.M.C.A. War Prisoners Aid), movies are proof that someone back home is thinking of them.

Army and Navy doctors have a word for movies. They call them "therapeutic stimuli." Someone has said that "one picture is worth a thousand aspirins." Field hospitals and rest camps welcome every film they can get (both the Red Cross and the USO are authorized to show them). Sometimes pictures have been projected on the ceiling for bedridden patients. In India, a whole show was run off for one wounded man.

At Bougainville, battle shock was counteracted by a tent theater that showed movies day and night. Men would come in from the firing line and see a feature picture. Probably few knew later what they had seen, but that didn't matter; it was a movie. It gave them a chance to regain balance.

One thing is certain: whatever they saw, it was not about war. War movies do not appeal to fighting men. Nor do Westerns. Men who have seen real shooting do not seem to care for the synthetic variety.

The Army has made many surveys of soldier tastes. Every picture shown overseas has been reported on by the officer handling films for his unit. These collected reports of audience reactions guide the OMPS selection board—six Army and Navy officers and two civilians—in their choice of 156 feature pictures a year from the industry's annual output of four or five hundred. Servicemen prefer musicals, comedies, mysteries, romantic dramas, documentaries, newsreels showing authentic war action. Best of all are movies whose components—street scenes, normal people on the streets, women who look like mothers, wives, sweethearts—bring them near home. One sergeant wrote in:

"When you look at a familiar actor or actress on the screen, it's just like walking . . . into the parlor of your own home, or sitting down to your own dinner table. It really does something for you."

Comments like that explain the fact that the 16-mm. films have been sent out with top transportation priorities. They indicate why films have been dropped by parachute to jungle troops, carried by pack mule to isolated mountain units, run in by PT boat to advance island posts. When Gen. George S. Patton's men were hurtling across France toward Germany, one projection team chased them for three days to show the latest picture.

Movies also help servicemen play host to friendly neighbors in areas around their posts. In the China-Burma-India Theater, relations between the Army and nearby mission schools were cemented by a showing of The Song of Bernadette. At Russian shuttle-bombing bases, American soldiers who had been entertained by the Red Army reciprocated with screenings of Hollywood films; the Americans translated the dialogue aloud to their guests. At a Persian Gulf base, Polish refugees were overwhelmed when they were invited to see their first American movie in several years. In Panama, native Indians who had never even heard of motion pictures quickly became regulars at free camp showings.

There have even been instances of "gatecrashing" by enemy troops. At an outdoor show on a South Pacific island, a soldier, lighting a cigarette, was startled to see the man beside him was a Jap (who was promptly imprisoned). In Italy, a German sniper was caught in a tree with his eyes riveted on a movie's open-air screen.

The basic purpose of all this film fare for servicemen is simple; it is to provide American entertainment for the Americans who need it most. That the purpose has been fulfilled, the Army and Navy will testify.

It was a soldier, Maj. Gen. Charles H. Bonesteel, who said, "Motion pictures are as necessary to the men as rations."

It was another soldier, Gen. Dwight Eisenhower, who included in his planning for the invasion of Europe one direct request: "Let's have more motion pictures."

Preparation for fun overseas: a bulletin is posted at an advanced American base in the South Pacific. If the enemy intervenes "theater" site is subject to abrupt change.

The audience (patients at a South Seas base hospital, in this case) gets ready. Pictures on these and on the next two pages are from the film-industry short, *Movies at War*.

The operator of a 16-mm. projector (foreground) sets up his machine in Italy. By the end of 1944, American troops overseas were using more than 5,000 projectors.

In New Guinea, as in New York, early birds at the show get the best seats. Natives made this grass-thatched stand to protect the screen against frequent jungle cloudbursts.

Youngsters in a liberated French town enjoy the show with their soldier hosts. The picture is untouched by Nazi hands—probably their first glimpse of that type in four years.

Frank Sinatra, a wartime phenomenon on the civilian front, also furnishes screen pleasure for a mixed audience of nurses and wounded men on a hospital ship at sea.

Below decks on a transport, returning from some fighting front, these wounded soldiers derive unconscious therapeutic benefit from merely watching an American-made movie.

Between bombing missions, Army Air Forces officers and men mingle at a North African airfield show. The seats aren't reserved, but there's lots of ground—free.

No better proof than this of what entertainment means to America's armed forces has come out of World War II, in which hours of boredom alternate with hours of peril.

The men are Navy pre-flight cadets, snapped during a USO Camp Shows performance at Chapel Hill, N. C. But the picture is symbolic. It could have been taken anywhere

on the six continents and numberless islands to which this conflict has sent our fighting men. The picture vividly illustrates the release from strain, the forgetfulness of self, that men must have to carry out the ugly, dirty, nerve-wrenching job of war. And it shows that release and forgetfulness can be bought with a simple coin: laughter.

CHAPTER VI

MIRROR OF BATTLE

On a Pacific island, American Marines make a heroic stand against overwhelming Japanese assaults. An American bomber screams to destruction over Europe, taking a Messerschmitt with it. Commandos raid a Norwegian coastal village, avenging helpless inhabitants victimized by the Nazis. In an African desert, Uncle Sam's soldiers fight to exhaustion and beyond, but vanquish the enemy before they drop . . .

These things have happened in the second World War, and they have happened all over again in fictional form on the motion picture screen, as they have in books and plays and radio programs. Behind these war pictures has lain the basic desire that motivates every studio production: to tell a good story with appealing characters and gripping action, a story well-written, well-directed, well-played.

With story value these screen dramas have tried to combine news significance. The Battle of Britain was mirrored in *Mrs. Miniver*. Russia's indomitable stand against Hitler found expression in *The North Star*. American fighting men on a dozen far-flung fronts have been glorified in *Wake Island, A Yank in the RAF, Guadalcanal Diary, Sahara, Bataan, Destination Tokyo, Action in the North Atlantic, The Eve of St. Mark*—the list goes on and on.

As might have been expected, some of these war pictures have been of high quality and some have been poor. Lacking realism and plausibility, the latter have been justly criticized, particularly by men who, to their cost, have learned what war really is.

War movies have had two special stimuli peculiar to them alone.

First was the tremendous public thirst for information about the war, even in re-enacted, edited and synthetic form.

Second was the morale job movies could do by showing audiences their sons and lovers in action, by spurring workers on the home front with visual evidence of the value of the weapons they made.

This morale factor explains why, early in the war, the armed services offered to cooperate with Hollywood in the production of war films. Gladly accepting their advice, the studios received, in addition, much more tangible help.

Consider, for example, the making of Moss Hart's *Winged Victory* by 20th Century-Fox (with all profits going to Army Relief).

During the filming, the Army sent no less than 14 technical advisers—all of them officers—to Hollywood. Among these advisers were experts on physical training, pressure chambers, and cadet-graduation exercises, as well as a WAC lieutenant, a flight surgeon, a chaplain, and several pilots with considerable combat experience.

The studio was given the use of facilities at seven different Army posts and air bases. At various times and places it was able to borrow — among other military items — 27 Liberator bombers, 55 basic trainers, six Higgins boats, 40 antiaircraft guns, 90 oil drums, 75 trench knives, 330 cartridge cases and such miscellany as crash trucks, ambulances, jeeps, walkie-talkies, rifles, parachutes and power cranes.

In addition, 400 inductees at one camp were held there additional days because the studio needed retakes and added scenes. More than 2,000 men paraded for the cameras; as many were assembled for a mass calisthenics scene. Twenty Air Forces cadets showed how a pressure chamber worked; another 360 were available for scenes of graduation exercises. All told, the studio was furnished a cast of thousands of men and equipment which was worth more than its own entire assets.

This sort of help has also been furnished on other productions, though generally on a less elaborate scale. It accounts for the unprecedented scope of many of Hollywood's war films.

Actual choice of stories for filming has been the studios' own responsibility. As with non-war pictures, ideas have usually originated in studio story departments, which cull all possible written sources of screen material—magazines, books, plays. Many of these are received in the form of manuscripts or advance proofs; others are brought to the studios' attention by agents.

Hollywood has bid heavily on books relating to the war — Ted Lawson's *Thirty Seconds over Tokyo*, John Hersey's *A Bell for Adano*, Richard Tregaskis' *Guadalcanal Diary*. One studio went up to $300,000 to get John Steinbeck's *The Moon Is Down*.

Firsthand accounts of the war have also found an avid market. Capt. Eddie Rickenbacker was deluged with offers for the screen rights to the story of his 21 days adrift in the Pacific. The parents of the five Sullivan brothers, who were lost with their ship, agreed to let the heroic saga be retold in film. Screen rights for Col. R. L. Scott's *God Is My Co-Pilot* (see p. 126) were purchased even before the book was marketed.

In every case where a story concerned any branch of the armed forces, permission to make the film had to be obtained from the War or Navy Department, which also reserved the right to reject any prepared script. The picture often had to be cleared with other Government agencies as well, for example, the State Department and the Office of Censorship.

The necessity of satisfying so many interested agencies helps to explain why war movies—those, that is, concerned with troops and shooting—constituted less than ten per cent of Hollywood's total output in the three years following Pearl Harbor. Another restraining factor is the public: despite its interest in combat stories, it can absorb just so many in a year. Timeliness also enters. When months may be involved in the production of a single picture, prime interest in any given war theater can, and often does, disappear before a film based upon it can be made and exhibited.

Finally there is the question of cost. Even with full Government co-operation, most war movies have cost at least a million dollars to make, sometimes two million.

The sweep and scope of these pictures require outdoor locations. Miracles can be wrought in studio oceans; special-effects men can do wonders with miniatures. But the panoramic view of a beach—with Higgins boats plowing through the waves, a convoy in the background, planes roaring overhead and a thousand armed troops wading ashore—obviously takes space. It also means transporting cast and equipment perhaps hundreds of miles, consuming costly time setting everything up, then perhaps waiting helplessly for good weather.

That was why the services lent a colossal hand on one scene from *Guadalcanal Diary*, which was filmed on the beach at a Marine camp near San Diego, with Marines filling in on the crowd scenes, the Navy supplying the convoy and small boats, the AAF the planes. Without such help, the studio could never have afforded to make the picture. It was a good investment for the services, though. The Marines set up recruiting stations near theaters where the film played and secured 12,000 recruits.

Most of Hollywood's top war films have dealt with battles, but others have probed into the background of World War II. Here is a scene from the picture, *The Seventh Cross,* grim tale of seven anti-Nazis who flee a German concentration camp in 1937. Six are caught; one (Spencer Tracy, left) escapes to go on fighting totalitarianism.

Charlie Chaplin's *The Great Dictator* used ridicule as a weapon against Fascism. Released a year before Pearl Harbor, it starred Chaplin and Jack Oakie (above) as a burlesque Adolf Hitler and Benito Mussolini. Proof of the film's power: democratic audiences loved it, movie-goers in Axis and some neutral nations were forbidden to see it.

One Hollywood feature film which was built entirely on fact was *The Hitler Gang*. Research was painstaking; it included material gathered by a former Nazi storm trooper. Unknown actors, chosen for resemblance to Nazi leaders, made up the cast. The story is that of Hitler (Robert Watson, above) and his rise to absolute power in Germany.

Although press, radio, and newsreels detailed Britain's lone stand against the Axis after Dunkirk, that epic event hit many Americans hardest in the fictional *Mrs. Miniver*. Starring Greer Garson and Walter Pidgeon, the film focuses on one English family. Through them it shows how all Britain was able to survive its most perilous days.

In Which We Serve awarded the British Navy its just share of glory. Written, directed, and produced in England by playwright Noel Coward, this is the saga of a warship from keel-laying to heroic destruction in battle—and of the men who love her. Here, survivors grimly watch their vessel sink. Author-actor Coward is at far right.

Flaming action on the beach at Dunkirk climaxes a film of air heroism, *A Yank in the RAF*. Made with the co-operation of the British, Canadian, and American Governments, the picture also includes sequences of actual British planes fighting over Germany. This was among the first feature films showing American audiences this aspect of war.

In 1941-43, while the Allies gathered strength to reconquer Europe from Hitler, the British harassed the enemy with frequent and far-famed raids on Nazi-held coastal points. *Commandos Strike at Dawn* recreates that type of raid; here, a Norwegian patriot (Paul Muni) guides the Tommies as they creep up on his home village.

This was the first major picture made in its entirety away from a studio. Cast, camera crews, and equipment were sent 1,400 miles to Vancouver Island, British Columbia, to get proper backgrounds. Canadian, British, Norwegian, and American Governments helped with the production. The result was a fictional war film realistic in every detail.

China's prolonged struggle against the Japanese invader has not been overlooked by Hollywood. Pearl Buck's *Dragon Seed* was put on the screen after two years of careful preparation (including creation in California of 100 acres of Chinese hills, farms rice fields). Above: a Chinese woman die: at Japanese hands to save her children

Russia's war travail, too, has had serious Hollywood consideration. This scene from *The North Star* (showing Red cavalrymen and guerrilla fighters battling to save a town from the Nazis) symbolizes the picture's message: that the Russians fought Germany not primarily to defend Communism but because of their fierce love of home and soil.

Of all American war films, none records a more moving drama than that based on the true story of Dr. Corydon Wassell. A missionary, he helped evacuate wounded from Java under Japanese attack, found himself a hero at home. Later, produced by Hollywood, *The Story of Dr. Wassell* became a screen vehicle for Gary Cooper (at right).

In *Wake Island,* Brian Donlevy (right) is one of 400 Marines cut off by the Japanese on a tiny Pacific island after Pearl Harbor. The film describes the death-stand of that gallant band, a tale of courage unparalleled in American history. Made in co-operation with the Marine Corps, this film is as factual a war movie as Hollywood has produced.

Another Marine saga—the daring assault of Lt. Col. Evans Carlson and his Raiders on Jap-held Makin Island in 1942—is commemorated in *Gung Ho!* Above, the head Raider (Randolph Scott, center) directs the landing party. Six of the real Carlson Raiders took part in this largely true-to-life picture, and Carlson himself acted as technical adviser.

First studio feature to utilize fighter pilots' conversation recorded in actual combat, *Wing and a Prayer* portrays an unidentified American aircraft carrier before and during the battle of Midway. (Above: one of our planes is forced down at sea.) Director and camera crew spent seven weeks aboard a real carrier, exposed 50,000 feet of film.

A fictional plot with a realistic background makes *Sahara* a gripping war film. It deals with one of the first American tank crews attached to the British Eighth Army during the North African retreat to El Alamein, Egypt; Humphrey Bogart is the tank commander. Here, Bogart's crew has shot down a Nazi plane and is taking the pilot prisoner.

Action in the North Atlantic shows American convoys in the thick of the 1942 U-boat campaign. Humphrey Bogart and Raymond Massey (above) play the mate and captain of a torpedoed tanker (it was built on the studio lot). By picturing the Merchant Marine, Hollywood has fully rounded out its coverage of our fighting units in this war.

By combining fact and fiction, Hollywood has produced many dramatically powerful movies to vivify the war for the American people. Pictures on these and following pages show in detail how one such movie, *God Is My Co-Pilot*, was made. Based on Col. Robert L. Scott's best-selling book of the same title, it describes his experiences

as a "Flying Tiger" one-man air force, and as commander of Maj. Gen. Claire Chennault's China Air Task Force. In the panoramic view above, cameras grind while Col. Scott's own P-40 swoops over hilly country near Hollywood—screen version of a foray in which Scott made three passes at a Japanese convoy, and killed hundreds of the enemy.

This is not realism; it's actuality. In a plane like these shown at a AVG base in China, Scott downed 13 enemy aircraft. Wounded, he pondered the words of an American missionary: "Son, you're not up there alone; you have the greatest co-pilot in the world."

Back in America, Scott (center) was interviewed with other air heroes at a New York movie première, later went on a war-plant pep-talk tour for Army Public Relations. A minister heard him speak, urged him to write a book, introduced him to a publisher.

The book agreed on, Scott dictated steadily for 72 hours, didn't like the result, rewrote it in off-moments from Army duty. Published in July, 1943, it soon sold more than 150,000 copies. Warner Bros. had read it in manuscript, paid $100,000 for movie rights.

Studio work on *God Is My Co-Pilot* started with research. Endless facts were gathered; Scott himself gave technical advice.

Dramatizing Scott's factual narrative was the job of three script writers. Peter Milne (above) spent three solid months on it.

Meanwhile the crafts shop was making items not otherwise obtainable—Japanese weapons and planes, bamboo furniture.

The wardrobe room supplied uniforms and other costumes, taking some from stock, renting others, tailoring the rest.

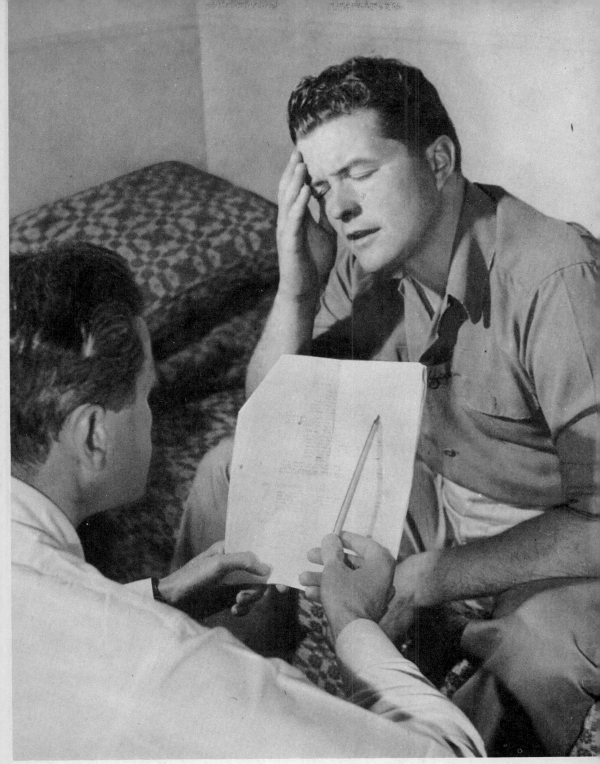

Actor Dennis Morgan, cast as Col. Scott, rehearses lines with the dialogue director. Scott said Morgan was ideal: young enough to be a convincing fighter pilot, perceptive enough to act with restraint. Alan Hale won the part of the priest known as "Big Mike."

Art director John Hughes (left), Scott (center) and director Robert Florey go over a map of China. Hughes designed sets for the film, made sketches and scale models, got them approved for cost, passed them on to studio carpenter, plaster and paint shops.

This miniature set of the air base at Kunming, China, was so realistic it made Scott "a little homesick." Sets were based on photographs supplied by Scott and Gen. Chennault. The film required 10,000 different "props"—from bombing planes to matches.

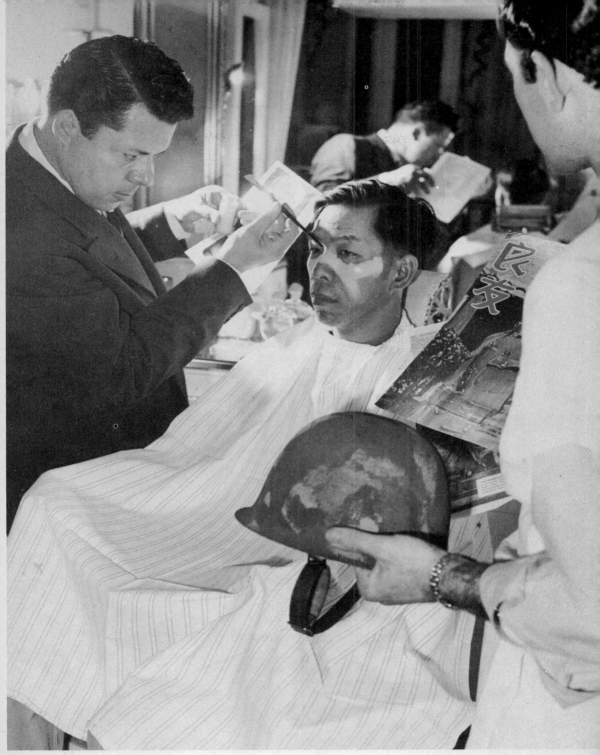

Elaborate make-up tests were part of the 16 months of preparation for actual filming of *God Is My Co-Pilot*. Here, Perc Westmore experiments on one of the 450 Chinese "extras" who balked when asked to portray Japanese soldiers but were finally persuaded.

236. CLOSEUP   SCOTT IN P-40

as he looks down below at the twisting Burma Road, then starts suddenly as he spots something.

237. FULL SHOT   EXT. THE BURMA ROAD   AN ANGLE PAST SCOTT
                                            IN THE P-40

A Jap troop column marches along a narrow, winding mountain road, behind a line of trucks. On one side is a sheer drop into the ravine below; on the other the steep wall of the mountain.

238. MOVING CLOSE SHOT   SCOTT IN P-40

His face tightens as he turns on his gun switches, glues his eye to the lighted sight and puts the nose of his ship over for a screaming dive.

239. LONG SHOT   SHOOTING AT SKIES   SCOTT'S P-40

goes into a dive, coming to CAMERA.

240. MOVING SHOT   THE JAP COLUMN   AN ANGLE FROM THE FRONT
     OF THE COLUMN   CAMERA ON DOLLY

Entirely unsuspecting, the Japs are singing one of their marching songs as they move along in a slow route step.

241. FULL LONG SHOT   JAP COLUMN ON BURMA ROAD

(The destruction of the Jap column should be SHOT and edited at a MONTAGE pace.)

Suddenly Scott's P-40 roars out of the clouds and jumps them from the rear. Swooping low with his six fifties spitting lead, he strafes the whole column from rear to front. Japs go down like flies. Some of the trucks in the van of the column start burning.

242. CLOSER ANGLE   TRUCKS BURNING OR EXPLODING

243. MED. SHOT   INSIDE COCKPIT   SCOTT IN THE P-40

Grinning from ear to ear, Scott banks the plane to for another pass at the Japs. He noses the plane for another dive.

A typical page from the script illustrates the minute attention to detail necessary to film action properly. Camera directions shown here took form in the scene on opposite page. This sequence, running only three minutes on the screen, was weeks in the making.

This Burma Road scene was shot 33 miles from the studio. Other footage was made at Luke Field, Ariz. (near Phoenix). The Army lent planes for air sequences, used prints of aerial shots for training films. Pilots were carefully briefed on camera positions.

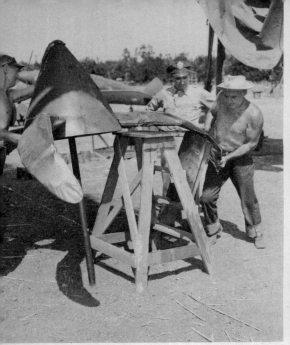

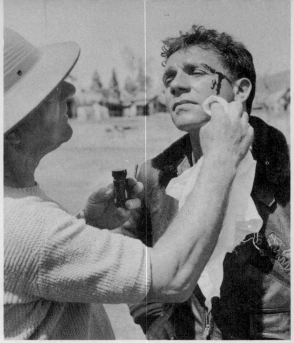

Two planes salvaged from junk heaps were "wrecked" in the picture. Here propeller blades are bent for a crash scene.

The fighter pilot (Dane Clark) "killed" in the crash is made up beforehand. Method of simulating blood is a secret.

Ready for the "take," Clark steps briefly before the camera while film title and scene number are recorded for reference.

Clark's plane is moved into position for a close-up after his "crash" was photographed. Air guns kick up a heavy dust.

This pictures the burial of another fighter pilot. While reflectors focus sunlight on the action, "rain" is sprayed over the actors from a hose. During shooting of the sequence, the ground got so mud-slippery that actors and crew could hardly stand.

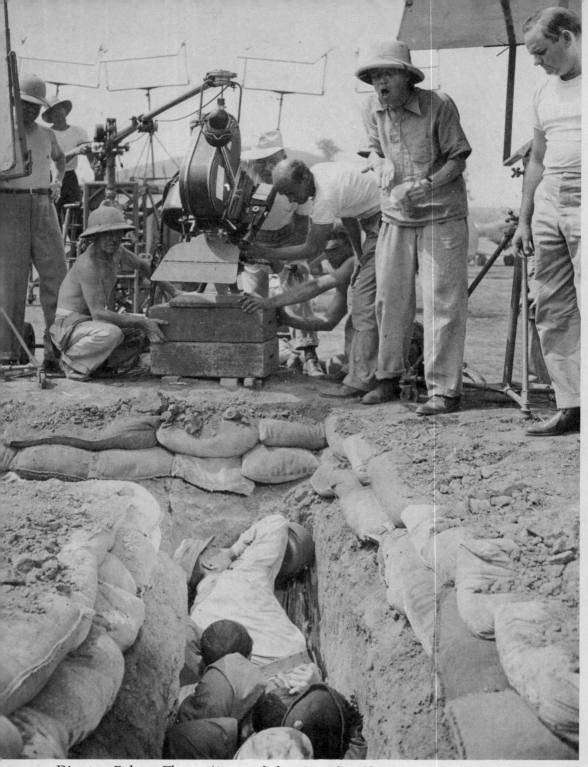

Director Robert Florey (in sun helmet) coaches extras for a scene in which Japanese bombers roar over a trench filled with pan- icky Chinese. He is telling them to act frightened, keying them up with rapid-fire chatter for the sequence to be photographed.

Lunchtime on location meant a hearty meal for workers on *God Is My Co-Pilot*. Here extras and a bit player (in flying gear) eat from trays they have brought to an outdoor table. More prominent members of the company usually ate in a shed, out of the sun.

Part of the time during filming, temperature was 110 in the shade. Here extras and workers cool off after lunch; for the "big names," cold drinks were served every half-hour. The company on location at Luke Field also reported fierce heat, ranging to 123 degrees.

When a scene called for exploding machine-gun bullets, the effect was produced by setting off explosive caps laid in the ground. Here workers are wiring caps and putting them in place. When cameras turned, controlled timing exploded them on schedule.

More preparation for shooting: Dennis Morgan (left) and Raymond Massey (cast as General Chennault) receive a last touch of make-up in a slit trench. Producer Robert Buckner felt that Massey would reflect Chennault's inner strength. Scott agreed.

This picture looks past the director's shoulder as Morgan acts out a trench scene. As Col. Scott, he is "sweating it out" on the ground during an aerial dogfight between AVG fighters and enemy bombers. The explosion is a simulated Japanese bomb hit.

Chinese extras here ride Morgan on bamboo chair during parade (which is pictured on the opposite page). They are celebrating his return after his plane was forced down, and he had been missing five days. As many as 427 extras appeared in one scene of picture.

142

On the screen, Chinese guerrillas parade at Kunming. Actually, this night parade sequence was made at the Warner Bros. ranch near Hollywood. By contrast with the days, the nights were so cold that technicians at times had to wrap themselves in blankets.

Dance director LeRoy Prinz was called in for certain Chinese dance scenes. Here he explains proposed camera angles to crew.

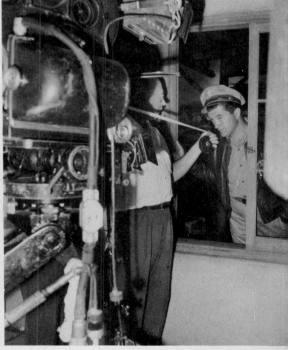

Dennis Morgan submits to a familiar routine—is measured for a close-up. *God Is My Co-Pilot* was his 14th starring picture.

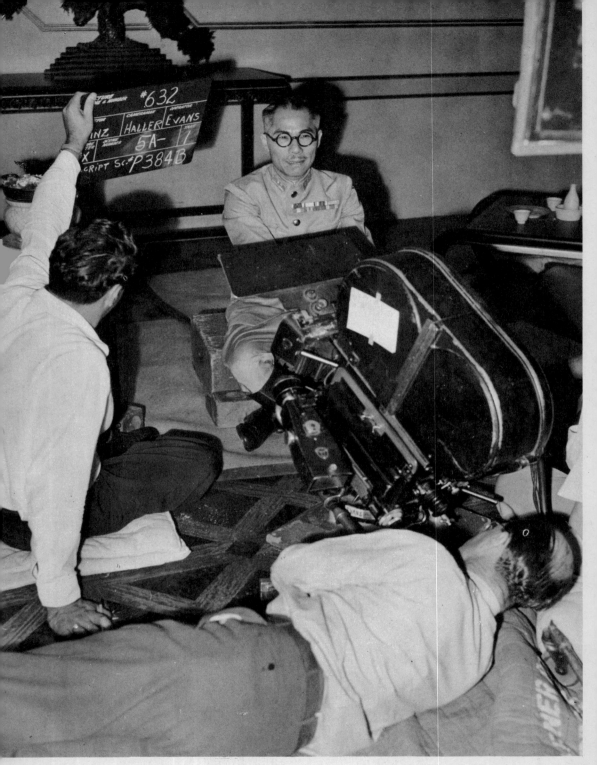

Typical of the Chinese who were willing to play Jap parts was Paul Fung, here posing for a close-up as General Kitchibura. Japanese insignia on his uniform were made and checked by experts—an example of the care taken by Hollywood to insure authenticity.

This "Chinese soldier," actually a Filipino, Eddie Lee, reads an American comic book between takes. Extras spent spare time playing gin rummy, grumbled over distance from Hollywood to location. Chinese men often played a game called Shop Ng Woo.

Following normal procedure, the film was completed and edited before dialogue, music and sound effects were cut in. Realism supplied by the sound-effects department included sounds of walking feet, gunfire, airfield sirens, explosions, other happenings.

When the picture was ready, studio officials planned ways to publicize it. Here Jack L. Warner (right), vice-president and executive producer of Warner Brothers, confers with his two top publicity men: Mort Blumenstock (left) and S. Charles Einfeld (center).

146

And, finally, the culmination of 16 months of preparation, 12 weeks of filming, the concentrated efforts of hundreds of people, the close co-operation of the Army, and the expenditure of hundreds of thousands of dollars: a top war movie is shown to the public.

CHAPTER VII

WITH GUN AND CAMERA

Wherever Americans have fought in this war, one uniformed figure has become familiar. He has stormed beaches with the Marines, slogged through mud with the Army, ridden Navy battlewagons and Coast Guard cutters, patroled the skies in fighting planes. Over one shoulder he carries a gun; over the other, a movie camera.

He is the combat photographer, trained to shoot Germans, Japs—and pictures. Thanks to him, the second World War has been the most thoroughly photographed in history. His continuing record of combat action has given our armed forces material for valuable training films, for detailed study by commanding officers, and for a permanent pictorial history of the war.

And his on-the-spot pictures, augmenting those of civilian newsreel cameramen, have helped immensely to clarify global war for the movie-going public. Millions of Americans have seen such service-produced feature films as *The Liberation of Rome* (see page 166), *At the Front in North Africa*, *Attack! The Battle For New Britain* (Army Pictorial Service); *The Memphis Belle* (Army Air Forces); *With the Marines at Tarawa* and *The Battle for the Marianas* (both filmed by the Marine Corps, edited in Hollywood); *The Battle of Midway* (Navy and the Office of Strategic Services).

All these combat reports, released through the motion picture industry's War Activities Committee, had wider and speedier runs in American theaters than commercial films have ever achieved.

Long before America entered the war, filmdom was aiding the armed services by setting up photographic units for the multi-million forces in training to fight on land, at sea and in the air.

First, hundreds of the industry's cameramen and other skilled studio workers—directors, writers, cutters, sound technicians—went into uniform to put their experience to direct use. Second, the studios began to train other servicemen to handle a movie camera.

As the services expanded their own facilities, the industry's part in the program became less direct. Training of photographers was centered in three schools; at Long Island City, N. Y. (Army Signal Corps), Pensacola, Fla. (Navy), and Quantico, Va. (Marine Corps). Some of the instructors came from permanent military personnel. More were reserves drawn from the motion picture industry and from magazines and newspapers.

The service schools give 17-week courses combining classroom and field work with basic military training. Students learn simple and advanced camera techniques, how to care for their equipment under conditions ranging from arctic to tropic. They learn to use carbine, automatic, submachine gun—

and to take care of themselves under fire. They cover maneuvers, learn to make instant decisions when hesitation may mean loss of an irreplaceable picture.

Many of them become still photographers or laboratory experts. Of those who specialize in motion picture work, the majority are assigned to reconnaissance or to recording routine military activities.

But there remain ample combat cameramen to provide some of the clearest, most exciting, most informative film ever made. Combat photographers recorded the appalling aftermath of the Japanese sneak attack on Hawaii. Since then they have covered all of the war's major military operations.

These battle sequences are sometimes made into feature films like *Tarawa*, but often woven into regular newsreel presentations. Audiences have watched them with little concept of the painstaking care that has gone into their production.

For example, long before our June, 1944, invasion of France, the Army Pictorial Service disposed photographic units among the assault troops so that every important action would be recorded. Navy camera units worked closely with the Army Pictorial Service and with the communications section of Supreme Headquarters. Every camera which could be bought or borrowed was mounted on landing craft, tanks and planes, or given out to cameramen.

During D-day alone, hundreds of thousands of feet of film were exposed. Air Forces cameramen covered the invasion from the sky, the Navy shot trans-Channel convoy operations, automatic cameras on the first boats ashore recorded the assault. Army and Navy cameramen ranged all over the beaches and they moved inland with the advancing Allied troops.

All negative film was returned to England, then flown to the United States for developing and cutting. Less than 60 hours after Normandy was invaded, Americans saw the event in newsreels.

Although Normandy required history's largest photographic operation, other combat films have depended on similar planning, and many have called forth a special kind of bravery from the men who shot them. In making *Tunisian Victory,* for example, four photographers were killed, four. gravely wounded (two of the latter were decorated for heroism). This feature film covered six months of fighting in North Africa, from the first Allied landings to the defeat of the Germans in Tunisia. It was produced jointly by film units of the American and British armies under Col. Frank Capra (in peacetime a Hollywood director) and Col. Hugh Stewart.

Marine combat photographers, who go through the mill of regular "boot" training before ever touching a camera, have been in some of the most ticklish spots of the war. Sgt. Bert Balaban, standing over the open hatch of a Liberator above Wake Island, lost his balance when ack-ack fire sent the plane zooming. With no parachute, with one foot in space, he grabbed a support with one hand, gripped his camera with the other, recovered his balance after a breathless moment. Then he went on shooting the raid, as most of his equipment fell on the Japs. On Tarawa, Sgts. Norman Hatch and Obie Newcomb had cameras hurled from their hands by the bodies of two of their buddies, shot by the enemy; they picked up rifles, joined the melee, later went back to making movies. On Saipan, Cpl. Arthur J. Kiely, Jr., took some excellent footage during one six-hour advance; but he had to stop three times to kill Japanese.

The Navy has had 11 combat-photography units in action in addition to its other motion picture crews. Each includes two movie men, one still man, an officer in charge. Most of these combat units have been in the Pacific. One Naval cameraman, Lt. Dewey Wrigley, began by filming the Army's recapture of Attu in the Aleutians; was sent to the Mediterranean and covered the invasion of Sicily; was aboard two vessels hit by the Germans and spent 15 hours in the sea; accompanied the first Army company to enter Rome and was nicked by a sniper's bullet; recovered, and filmed the Allied landings in Southern France.

Combat photographers have fallen on the bloody ground of Africa, Europe, Asia. They have been lost at sea, shot down from the sky. But they have gone after their pictures and their pictures have come back.

The battle of Tarawa was one of the many epic events of World War II recorded in detail by combat photographers. Marine cameramen brought back 5,000 feet of battle film, from which was made the first movie to show the American public an entire Pacific operation. Here a photographer (fourth from right) "shoots" a direct assault being made

on a bomb-proof Japanese blockhouse. The
picture illustrates dramatically the hazards
that these cameramen confront. Of the 15
cameramen under Capt. Louis Hayward,
the former movie star, two were killed and
one was wounded. The cameramen went in
with the first waves, often had to drop
their cameras to fight for their lives.

Besides picturing actual battle scenes, combat photographers must have a reportorial approach to "names that make news." Here an Army lensman films Gen. George S. Patton, Jr. (second from left), wading ashore at Gela, Sicily. Patton was preparing to take command of American forces in our first invasion of European soil (July, 1943).

In a rubble-strewn street in Nettuno, Italy (February, 1944), an Army movie-maker is covering the house-to-house action. His camera comes up, focuses on a "duck" (amphibious truck) set afire by German shells. Thus he provides excitement for cinema-goers back home and, more important, something for Army supply officers to study.

PICO
alt. m. 190

Combat photographers were in company with the advanced troops as America's Fifth Army entered Pico, Italy, May 25, 1944. Here, the first cameraman to view the town keeps close to the buildings as a precaution against snipers. Note 16-mm. camera carried in right hand, and the first aid kit which is attached at the back of his belt.

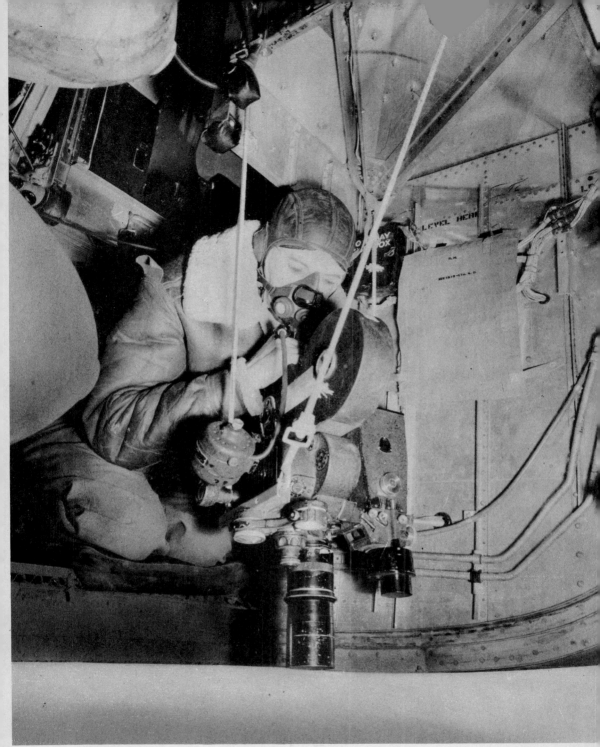

From the catwalk of a Liberator B-24 bomber a combat photographer aims his camera through the open bomb bay doors at the command, "Bombs away!" His camera, suspended by rubber shock cords from the top of the plane, is kept taut, can be tilted at will without vibration. This cameraman is tied securely by a cord around his waist.

The war and the combat cameraman have made this scene familiar to American movie audiences: the landing of troops and equipment on a hostile shore. Here the Navy photographer at left hit the beach early, and promptly set up tripod and camera to film the landing craft and their cargo of men, trucks, tractors, and supplies. The place:

Kiska Island in the Aleutians, where the Army and Navy arrived in August, 1943, only to find that the Japanese had fled. Yet the same scene has been repeated across the world on other shores where the enemy did give battle—and was beaten. By recording that scene, time on time, the combat photographers have shown us the shape of Victory.

Part 2: COMBAT CAMERAMAN AT WORK

This is the story of one Army combat photographer. He typifies the hundreds who joined one or another of the services to help film the second World War.

His name is Victor W. Groshon. He comes from Philadelphia, where he used to run a small photographic studio. In February, 1942, he enlisted in the Army. He was 29, a tall, lanky, rawboned fellow with no family to tie him down. Groshon told the recruiting officer he wanted to see some action.

At first he was sorry he'd mentioned his photographic background: they had him in the Signal Corps Photographic School at Fort Monmouth, N. J., taking cameras apart and putting them together, and that wasn't action. Fort Sam Houston, Tex., was no better. But then he learned that his outfit was going over. They left from Newport News in October and Groshon, a sergeant by that time, began to think that perhaps he'd see some action after all.

On November 7 he was sure of it. That was the day he watched Allied naval guns throw tons of steel at Fedalah, a fortified town on the coast of Morocco near Casablanca. A tank lighter dropped him in chest-deep water with his camera, 1,000 feet of film, two days' rations and a .45 revolver. Somehow Groshon kept everything dry until he reached the beach.

Night was falling; supplies were being unloaded in a chaos of shell craters. Groshon had orders to report to his lieutenant, but couldn't find him. About midnight, he stopped trying and simply went to sleep.

Next morning he was up at daylight, taking pictures. (He finally found his lieutenant.) All day there were German strafing attacks—dune-high flights so sudden a man couldn't get to cover. Groshon had wanted action. Now he was getting it, and getting some fine film footage, too. He even caught his own ship sinking in the harbor with a U-boat torpedo between her ribs.

In time things grew calmer, the French signed an armistice and Groshon moved into quarters in Casablanca. In January, 1943, he covered the Roosevelt-Churchill conference there. Then he marked time until he was sent to Tunisia to help record the last days of Rommel's *Afrika Korps*.

One day that Groshon remembers was Easter Sunday, 1943. There was an outdoor church service near Mateur, and he was up in a tree filming it. Suddenly there was a whistle, an explosion; everyone but the chaplain fell flat. Groshon was nearly shaken from his perch. It developed that they had been under direct observation of Germans entrenched on the famous Hill 609.

In May, Groshon was ordered to Army Pictorial Service headquarters at Algiers. There he spent several weeks working on plans for the invasion of Sicily. His job was to make pictures of sand models of the enemy-held coastline; such pictures were used by our pilots on D-day—July 10. Groshon was there that day himself, going in under fire again to land on a beach near Gela.

During the Sicilian landings he dodged repeated Nazi air attacks, got extraordinary pictures of a Liberty Ship exploding from a bomb hit. A few days later he was told to clean up (no easy task) and report to the square in the center of Gela. There he stood in line, at attention, as General Patton pinned the Legion of Merit on his chest (see page 165) for his work back at Fedalah. That was another day the sergeant remembers.

His next assignment was the dream of all combat photographers. With still cameraman Sgt. Jay Conley as a teammate, he was given a jeep, plenty of film and rations and ordered to go wherever he thought there might be pictures. The two wandered over Sicily, following the fast American campaign. In September they wandered right on over to Italy, and up the peninsula to Naples.

Groshon and Conley stayed in Italy eight months. During that time they covered several assignments, including five weeks on a pictorial record of churches and other historic monuments damaged in the fighting. Then the Army decided that Groshon's 19 continuous months in combat areas were enough. He was ordered back to the States.

Here he was assigned to the Signal Corps Photographic Center at Long Island City, N. Y. Groshon didn't mind. He'd come through without a scratch, and he'd seen all the action anyone could want.

In a re-enactment staged specially for this book, Sgt. Victor W. Groshon shows what combat photographers do during an amphibious landing. He is pictured in his place on the ramp of a Higgins boat, ready to leap out with the other men. His compact little motion picture camera is wrapped in a jacket for protection against the water.

On another boat (in the same wave as Groshon's) combat photographer Sgt. Bernard Haber thrusts his camera through an opening in the ramp to record action on the beach.

Groshon took this shot. It shows the unloading of supplies from a boat in the second wave. Some are coming in laden, others are slogging back empty-handed for more.

Enemy planes overhead! Groshon leaps for the safety of a machine gun emplacement. Combat photographers must take care of themselves first, and make pictures second.

Now the planes roar down the beach, spitting bullets. Crouched by his protecting sandbags, Groshon has split seconds to decide whether the raid should be filmed.

On another section of the beach, Sergeant Haber films action under cover of rifle fire. His helmet net subdues the sun's glare, lessens the chances of attracting a sniper.

With opposition on the beach ended, Gros- emergency medical treatment. The hurt man
hon focuses on a wounded soldier receiving will get further attention back on his ship.

Another casualty provides still another subject for Groshon's lens. Such pictures are of general public interest, may also be used for instruction by the Medical Corps.

No re-enactment, this—Sergeant Groshon re-
ceives the Legion of Merit Ribbon from
General Patton. This was the first time decorations were awarded to our troops in Europe.

Part 3: "THE LIBERATION OF ROME"

Outstanding among service-produced feature pictures of the second World War is *The Liberation of Rome*, compiled from footage shot by combat photographers of the combined Allied services in Italy. It appeared in 11,875 theaters in 16 weeks following Rome's fall. It covers nine months of fighting. On these and following pages appear scenes from the film. The captions are based on the original narration. Above: *The victorious Allied Fifth Army enters Rome on June 4, 1944.*

For the invasion of Italy the Allied Chiefs of Staff had conceived a two-part plan. The first part entailed control of the Mediterranean, capture of the Foggia airfields, the draining of Nazi strength from other areas and Italy's surrender. Part 1 began at dawn on September 3, 1943, as shown above. The British Eighth Army crossed the narrow strait from Sicily to debark on the toe of the Italian boot. Five days later, Italy's capitulation was announced. Then the Italian fleet surrendered.

But the Germans in Italy had not surrendered. On September 9, the Fifth Army
(made up of American and British troops) stormed ashore at Salerno, near Naples.
It was supported by massed airpower. Yet it found the going hard.

This captured German film shows how strongly the Nazis resisted. From high
ground, overlooking the harbor and beaches, they raked the landings with 88-mm.
guns. But finally the Fifth Army, and units of the Eighth, forced them to fall back.

Here is one of Hitler's airfields at Foggia (on the east coast) as it looked when the Eighth Army captured it. Possession of Foggia made the Allies' Mediterranean shipping relatively safe, enabled them to bomb the enemy anywhere in the Balkans.

On October 1, 22 days after the landings at Salerno, the Fifth Army entered Naples, one of the world's great ports. Damage done by the Nazis was soon repaired, and Naples became the main port of supply in Italy.

From Naples on, the going was tougher. A month after Salerno, Allied forces reached the Volturno River, were slowed by mountains, autumn torrents, rain. Men of the Fifth Army sometimes clung to their positions 30 days without relief.

This is a soldier wounded near the Volturno. At times the advance in this sector was at the cost of a man a yard. But the Fifth came through, the first army in history to conquer Italy through these mountains.

Meanwhile, to the east, the Eighth Army fought its way up the Adriatic. At the little town of Ortona the Canadians met desperate, determined German resistance. Tank battles and hand-to-hand fighting raged through the streets for 18 days.

At last Ortona fell. This dazed old man was left in the once gay town—left to wander forlornly through the war-torn streets. Outside Ortona the battle raged on;

the Germans were slowly pushed northward. Sometimes, for days at a time, the forces were deadlocked. But always the Nazis yielded in the end.

In the central sector, Mediterranean Commander Eisenhower (left) met with the Fifth Army's leader, Gen. Mark Clark. The Fifth had come only 12 miles in three months since crossing the Volturno. And at Cassino it was bogged down, stalemated.

To break the stalemate, the Allies tried an end run—amphibious landings at Anzio (above) and Nettuno. The Germans were caught off guard. For several days American and British troops encountered only light opposition.

Then the German leaders, Marshals Rommel and Kesselring, brought up 13 reserve divisions with heavy Luftwaffe support. This picture hints of the close, bloody fighting that followed their attempt to hurl us into the sea.

Despite all the enemy could do, the Fifth hung onto a hundred square miles of beachhead. But it paid a heavy price. The hospital ships were busy at Anzio. And hundreds of Americans went off to German prison camps.

Back at Cassino, the bitter deadlock continued ... Here the cameraman catches two British medical corpsmen going to the aid of a fallen soldier ...

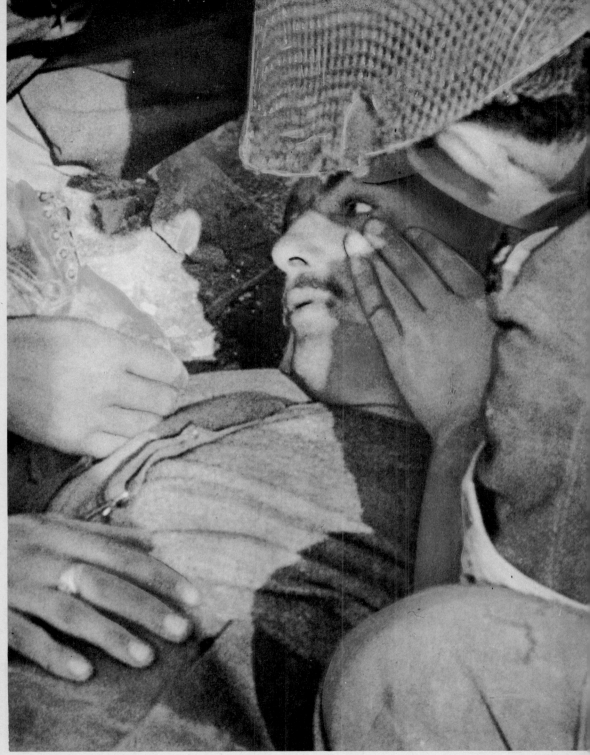

. . . and here, a few moments later, the soldier is being examined by the corpsmen. Aid is unavailing. He is dead.

At Cassino the Germans held an obvious advantage by their occupation of the Benedictine Abbey above the town. They were asked to abandon it, and they refused. There was no alternative but to bomb the Abbey to save soldiers' lives.

Italian friends,
BEWARE!

We have until now been especially careful to avoid shelling the Monte Cassino Monastery. The Germans have known how to benefit from this. But now the fighting has swept closer and closer to its sacred precincts. The time has come when we must train our guns on the Monastery itself.

This sequence details the destruction of the Abbey. A month later we dropped 1,144 tons of bombs on Cassino itself. The Germans hid in caves and tunnels, hung on like death. But Part 1 of the campaign was nearly over.

179

Part 2—the all-out assault to drive the Nazis from Italy—opened the night of May 11 as Allied guns split the darkness from Cassino west to the sea. Then the Fifth Army, reinforced with British, American, French, Polish troops, began to move.

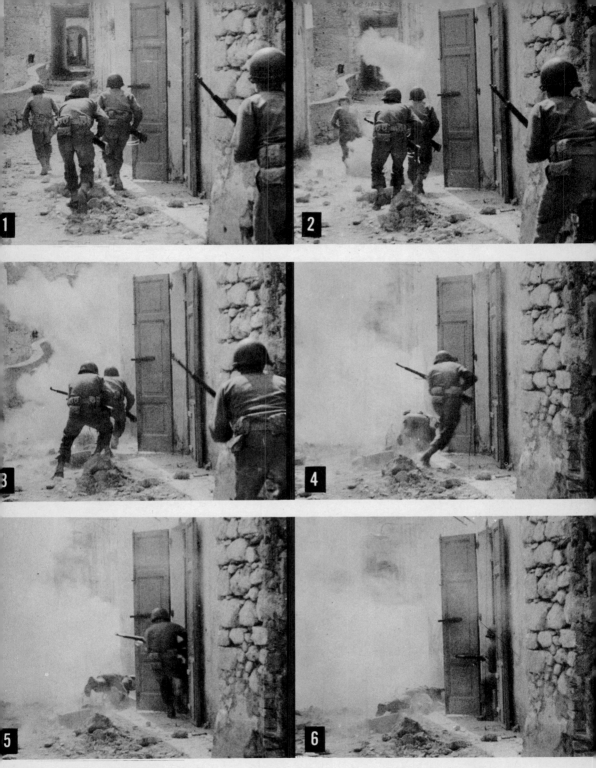

Here is action in Cassino. Allied troops are driving ahead—and some are dying—behind massed artillery and tanks. The enemy resisted, but the advance went on. Soon the Fifth made contact with the Anzio beachhead troops; the two forces merged.

Thousands of German troops were outflanked in the surging advance of the Allied forces. Prisoners were brought in on every sector of the front. They were beaten, exhausted, hopeless. These faces, with despair etched on them, show the plight of

Hitler's soldiers as they advanced under the white flag of truce. The road to Rome was lined with the wreckage of Nazi legions, blasted by Allied air power, as they fled before the reunited Fifth Army.

At last; on June 4, the Fifth Army entered Rome from the south. Cheering Italians lined streets from which the Germans had hastily fled northward.

And the Eternal City was free. After 21 years, a free Rome raised its voice in the public square. A free Rome read again, sang again, laughed again...

A free Rome gathered in the Piazza San Pietro to receive the Pope's blessing...

And, at once joyful over deliverance and sorrowful over casualties, prayed...

... remembering the dead—whose lives had been the price of Rome's liberation.

CHAPTER VIII

TWO ON THE AISLE

On the day Japanese bombers made their sneak attack on Pearl Harbor, a motion picture titled *Bomber* was playing in Honolulu.

This was a coincidence, but it underscores Hollywood's part in· our war effort. For *Bomber* was no melodramatic studio feature. Government-made, released through special agreement with motion-picture theaters, it explained factually and succinctly how medium bombers are produced, urged workers to get into this important phase of national defense.

That tragic Sunday the word "defense" was replaced by "war." But filmdom had already been in the fight for 18 months. Back in 1940, Hitler's lightning conquest of France had sent a chill of fear along American spines. The week the British evacuated Dunkirk, leaders of the industry signaled their awareness of the situation by forming the Motion Picture Committee Co-operating for National Defense.

The Committee had a patriotic program: to distribute, transport and exhibit, without cost, national-defense films produced by various Government bureaus. It was also candidly conscious of Hollywood's own stake in the peril threatening America. The late Sidney R. Kent, film executive, put it bluntly: "This job must be done just as efficiently and quickly as though we were doing it for ourselves—because, in fact, we are."

Action soon followed. Representing the nation's 16,486 motion-picture exhibitors, a sub-committee (headed by R. B. Wilby of Atlanta) undertook to approve pertinent Government-made war-information films and reject advertising films or those made simply to glorify Washington agencies. Filmdom also offered counsel and criticism based on contact with movie audiences.

Frequently this criticism had a salutary effect. Once a Government agent suggested a 20-minute film appealing to skilled workers to register with the U. S. Employment Service. The committee co-ordinator recalled that Lincoln's *Gettysburg Address* ran less than four minutes on the screen, asked if the proposed film were five times as important. As produced, the film ran 100 seconds.

Unfortunately, such careful scrutiny has not been given all war-information films. Although many have been highly interesting, some have been tedious.

One way such films served the defense effort was in recruiting volunteers for the armed forces as well as various types of workers for industry. *Winning Your Wings*, with James Stewart, and *Wings Up*, with Clark Gable, brought thousands of young men into the Army Air Forces. *Women in Defense*, a plea for women to enter industry or the voluntary services, was written by Mrs. Franklin D. Roosevelt and narrated by

Katharine Hepburn. Mrs. Roosevelt, then assistant director of the Office of Civilian Defense, vigorously edited the film after screening it in semi-final condition at the White House.

After Pearl Harbor, the Committee Co-operating for National Defense continued unchanged except in name. As the War Activities Committee—Motion Picture Industry, it renewed its pledge to the President of all-out co-operation. Then it rushed to the nation's screens a Red Cross appeal for additional public support.

The 100 or more Government information films exhibited in American theaters since we entered the war have covered a wide range: collection of fats, paper, copper, fuel; production, rationing and conservation of food; increased wartime taxes; American forces in action; recruiting for the WAC, WAVES, SPARS, Seabees, Cadet Nurses and Red Cross nurses' aides.

In 1944, when the WAC recruiting program was in the doldrums, Col. Oveta Hobby called on movie theaters for help. In 12 days audiences were seeing a recruiting trailer featuring Lionel Barrymore, supplementing a Signal Corps film and a commercial Technicolor short on the subject. The industry also pulled out its publicity stops with recruiting booths in theater lobbies; with stage shows featuring local beauties modeling WAC uniforms; with a mass induction of 100 WACs in Times Square.

Establishment of the Office of War Information in June, 1942, gave Washington a single centralized contact with movie producers, distributors and exhibitors. As the OWI set about driving home the implications of total war, films showing the courage of civilians in invaded countries alternated with combat reports on our own men and the weapons our workers were producing.

The first screen "communiqué" was the two-reel Technicolor film, *The Battle of Midway*, photographed by the Hollywood director, Cmdr. John Ford. The second was by Col. Darryl Zanuck (head of 20th Century-Fox), who led the unit which filmed *At the Front in North Africa*. As further service-produced films were finished, exhibitors showed them to U. S. audiences.

A year after the OWI was set up, Congress cut its budget for domestic films from $1,226,000 to $50,000, thus eliminating the OWI from the production end of the business. Said Senator Lodge of Massachusetts: "It is much better to have motion pictures made in Hollywood by moving-picture professionals ... than to have the Government itself try to make them." The industry promptly took over the production—gratis—of these war-information films.

Meanwhile, distribution and exhibition went on, with the accent on speed. Commercial short subjects take 18 months to play four to ten thousand theaters; war information shorts have played 13 to 15 thousand theaters in 18 weeks, brief screen bulletins (with simple appeals to buy War Bonds, donate blood, conserve fuel) in six weeks.

Release of the pictures has reflected the course of the war. In 1944, important victories were followed by a production letdown at home; hence, special shorts and bulletins were hurried to the theaters to help keep workers on the job. *The War Speeds Up*, made in 12 days by the Signal Corps to show the need of increased production, was released to theaters at the urgent request of Chief of Staff Marshall. When the European war reached its semi-final stages, *Target—Japan* (produced for the Navy by The March of Time) high-lighted the job still facing the Allies in the Pacific.

At the beginning of 1945, it appeared likely that, even when final victory came in sight, the industry's war role would continue. OWI director Elmer Davis has said that motion pictures must help make the "patched-up world hold together" by telling the public about international organization for peace, the care of veterans, post-war jobs, skyways of the future, and so on.

It has been suggested several times that the movies be used for commercial advertising on a national scale. The industry has always vetoed that suggestion; it has never been interested in turning the screen into a "circulation package." But this war has shown that it will go all out to advertise our national needs, and to "sell" 85,000,000 movie-goers information that can further our national welfare.

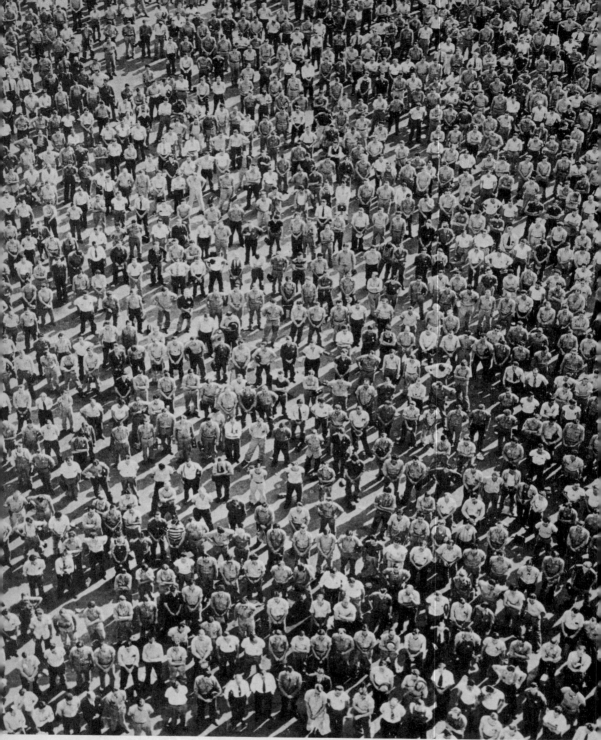

Typical of the short, hard-hitting wartime films made by the OWI was *Manpower*. Released in 1942 through the War Activities Committee, it called on America's working millions (symbolized in the scene above) to throw their productive might behind our fighting men. The picture played in 12,000 theaters to an estimated 25,000,000 persons.

War-information films also helped recruit men and women for the armed forces. A scene like this in the Navy's *Chief Neeley Reports to the Nation* is one example of a woman in uniform filling a man's job (as an aviation machinist's mate). When *Neeley* was shown, WAVES enlistments jumped from an average of 650 to 1,000 a week.

This is a scene from *Tanks,* one of several pictures made to lift war workers' morale by documenting the use of weapons they produced. With Orson Welles as narrator, it traces the progress of the M-3 medium tank from Detroit factory to delivery aboard a ship bound for combat. Similar films dealt with shipbuilding and bomber production.

Some films emphasized the fact that war workers should be loyal to their jobs. One, *Conquer By the Clock*, told the story of a lax girl who took time off for a smoke (above). In her hurry to leave her post she slipped an "inspected" sign in her box of bullets. Result: a defective bullet passed, a gun jammed, an American soldier was killed.

For several years the American Red Cross has made an annual screen report to its contributors. This picture (from *At His Side*) shows a Red Cross Clubmobile girl serving refreshments to soldiers in a remote Pacific outpost. Clubmobiles carry food, drinks, magazines, phonograph records, cigarettes, sometimes 16-mm. projectors and films.

When war's cost was reflected in 1942's increased income taxes, Walt Disney's *The New Spirit* explained their necessity. Above: Donald Duck, as a first-time taxpayer, wavers between his spendthrift and thrifty selves. Of 26,000,000 people who saw the short, polls showed one in three said it influenced their willingness to pay taxes.

Several Government agencies enlisted the screen's aid in dramatizing the importance of food as a weapon of victory. *Food for Fighters, Black Marketing, Food and Magic* (on conservation) were some of the shorts released. Typical food picture is *Farm Battle Lines*, which urges the farmer to stay on the farm and increase food production.

This picture of a soldier enjoying his chow, along with his book of comics, is from *Troop Train*, a film suggested by the Office of Defense Transportation. Produced by the OWI, the movie appealed to civilians to give up unnecessary travel. It depicted the transfer of an armored division by rail, showed why troops are given preference in wartime.

The Negro Soldier, a 40-minute odd-length feature, was produced by the U. S. Army Signal Corps, directed by Col. Frank Capra. It recounted the Negro's many services in America's former wars, his widespread contribution to this one. Although the film was made to be shown to Negro troops only, it merited, and got, national theatrical release.

What one war-swollen factory town did to relieve its crowding and traffic congestion was reported in *Community Transportation,* the story of Bridgeport, Conn. This scene illustrates the rush-hour throngs that made bus travel a nightmare; the film explains how Bridgeport staggered work hours and set up car pools—a lesson for other towns.

Get in the Scrap was another Walt Disney short featuring Donald Duck as an aroused patriot on the home front. In this one—as exemplified above—Donald became a collector of everything he could get hold of that would help the war effort. One result: Disney fans of all ages swelled movie house salvage collections with scrap of all kinds.

PRODUCED BY THE
BRITISH MINISTRY OF INFORMATION

"V-1"

Distributed by the
**WAR ACTIVITIES COMMITTEE—
MOTION PICTURE INDUSTRY**

Here are scenes from an information film, with captions based on its narration.

This is London during its grim ordeal—the 80-day robot-bomb blitz of 1944.

This is you as the V-1 might find you—any time, day or night, for 80 days.

You're an office worker coming home around six—and this is your home.

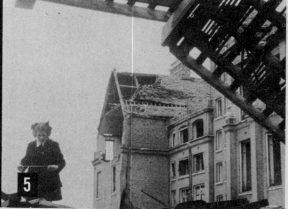

You're a passenger in a cross-town bus—and this is the end of your last trip.

You're a kid at school—and this is your lesson for the day.

6 You're a patient in a hospital—and this is your last treatment.

7 You're a worshiper in church—and this is where you kneeled and never got up.

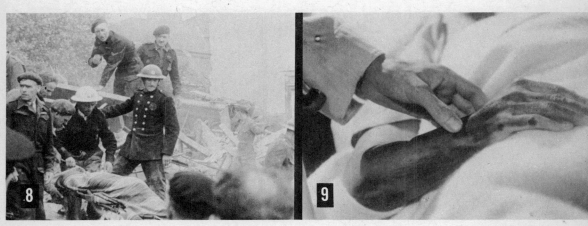

8 Yes, your London suffered: 23,000 buildings destroyed, 1,000,000 damaged . . .

9 . . . over 5,000 lives lost, over 16,000 broken. London suffered — and fought.

10 You're part of the crew of an ack-ack battery, and you can't close your eyes.

11 During the V-1 blitz ack-ack brings down more than 1,500 bombs.

12

You work hard down on the South Coast, in the white sun—and the nervous night.

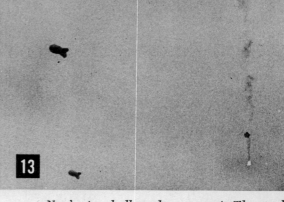

13

You're in a balloon-barrage unit. The steel cables down nearly 300 bombs.

14

You're the pilot of a Tempest or a Spitfire, screaming through space, and . . .

15

. . . planes bring down nearly 2,000 pilotless bombers in the 80 days.

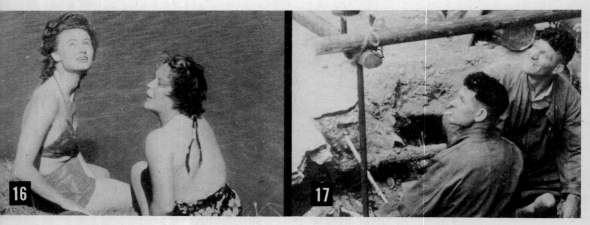

16

You're a hairdresser, nervously going in for a swim on Sunday afternoon.

17

You're a citizen of Southern England; it's a matter of life and death—yours.

You're a mother, watching your child blown to eternity by an insensate horror.

Schools, hospitals, churches, landmarks —these were high among Hitler's targets.

For, although half the 8,000 V-1's were brought down, the rest struck—hard.

But, though your city was hurt, it will live. Reconstruction has begun.

These children, like tens of thousands of others, are homeless. But . . .

. . . their city endures. And its future is the future of a noble nation.

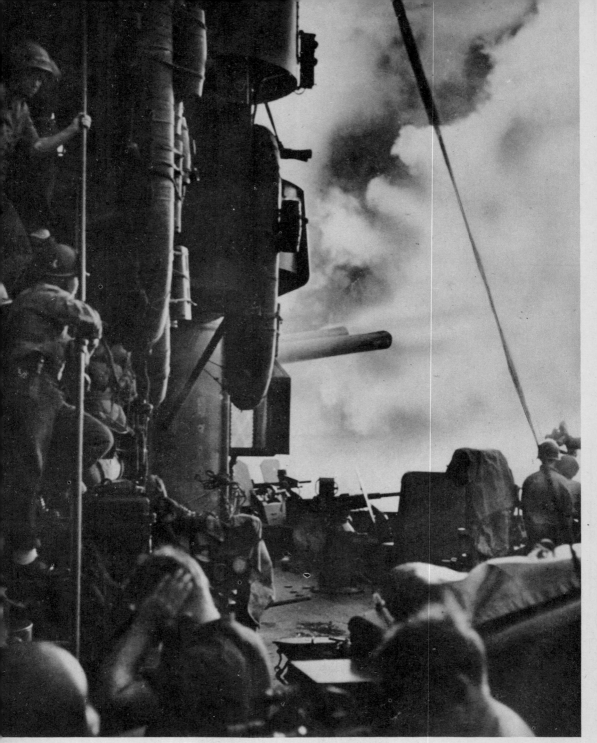

Two information films helped to rally the American people late in 1944, when over-optimism was unjustified by the uncertain march of events. *The War Speeds Up* showed how fast-moving operations in Guam, the Philippines, and France had created a critical shortage in certain weapons, importuned workers to stay on their jobs.

Target-Japan was requested by the Navy to remind the public that the war in the Pacific had only begun. Barring no holds, this showed the terrible cost (above) of our victories over the Japanese, stressed the price of other victories still to be won. In their sobering influence on national thought, such films as this fill a vital wartime role.

CHAPTER IX

BONDS, BLOOD AND BOUNTY

In the first World War, as persons of mature years like to recall, the sight of such beloved movie personalities as Marie Dressler, Douglas Fairbanks and Mary Pickford giving free shows stimulated the civilian war effort.

This time the exertions of the whole 240,-000 members of the motion picture industry, plus other thousands from allied entertainment fields, have elicited emphatic responses in bond purchases, blood donations and audience collections for war charities.

Ted R. Gamble, head of the U. S. Treasury's War Finance Division, which runs the War Bond campaigns, is himself the operator of motion picture theaters. In Portland, Oregon, Mr. Gamble put such enthusiasm into the job of signing up defense workers for ten per cent payroll deductions for bonds that Secretary of the Treasury Morgenthau brought him to Washington as an assistant. When the Government made its decision to keep bond buying on a voluntary basis, Ted Gamble quickly demonstrated that the public would respond willingly to showmanship and salesmanship.

To help finance the war, drain off surplus buying power, and avert inflation, more and more of the public's money had to be converted into bonds. Sales of small-denomination bonds to individuals played a big part in this job. Such sales increased from $1,600,000,000 in the First War Loan campaign to more than $5,500,000,000 in the Sixth. In the Fifth drive—coinciding with the invasion of Normandy — 72,113,000 "E" bonds, issued to individual investors only, were bought by 50,000,000 people, who still held $89 worth of bonds for every $100 invested in previous drives.

In 1941-42 Hollywood and the movie theaters had helped to popularize payroll deductions for bond purchases. September, 1942, *Salute to Our Heroes* month, saw a million additional factory workers signed up. In that campaign, 59 movie stars traveled 21,000 miles through the 48 states for bond rallies in 368 communities.

Many were the problems of the Hollywood bond salesmen. Oscar Doob, spark plug of the "Stars Over America" campaign, wrote during the thick of it: "We have been dealing with human beings who, unfortunately, get sick, change their minds, break hands, lose their bridgework, have livings to make, and are subject to draft call."

But the Hollywood touch spelled success. In Albuquerque, Ginger Rogers sold her dancing shoes for $10,000 in bonds. Someone in the crowd asked her to put up her hat, bought it for $50,000 in bonds, then returned it. Veronica Lake auctioned off a lock of her hair for $186,000 in bonds. One star auctioned off twelve "pet dogs" in as many days. In Portland, a young man used his life's savings to buy a $5,000 bond from Lana Turner, got a kiss, ran electrified to a recruiting station and joined the Navy.

Such incidents got more publicity than the stars' valuable heavy-duty trouping.

By 1944, when the Treasury launched three bond-selling campaigns, motion picture exhibitors were credited, directly or indirectly, with twenty per cent of "E" bond sales. Movie theaters emphasized direct sales to patrons. During the year more than 15,000 "Bond Premières" were held, with distributors supplying pictures without charge and exhibitors giving up cash admissions for audiences composed exclusively of bond buyers. On December 7, 1944, theaters commemorated Pearl Harbor by sponsoring a Free-Movie Day for bond purchasers. Proceeds topped all similar campaigns—in New York's metropolitan area alone, over 31,000 bonds were sold, valued at $1,598,610.

Showmanship continued to be filmdom's most important contribution to history's most gigantic war-financing program.

Broadway erected a four-story, ten-ton cash register in Times Square (see pages 212-13), with a galloping electric sign, a thunderous loud-speaker and a horde of clerks, performers and speakers who, for twelve hours daily, during four hectic weeks, sold better than a bond a minute. During the Sixth War Loan, at the end of 1944, a $40,000 replica of the Statue of Liberty replaced the cash register. President Roosevelt threw the switch to light the statue's torch.

Nor was the Treasury Department the only agency served by the motion picture theaters. Through them, the Red Cross, United Nations Relief, U.S.O., March of Dimes and Army-Navy Emergency Relief went directly to the hearts and pockets of audiences, who responded by giving $30,-000,000 to these causes during 1942-1944.

The record contribution was $6,793,000 to the Red Cross in 1944—a result of a national drive in movie theaters. Highlight of this campaign was a huge rally at Madison Square Garden, New York, with more than a thousand stars of stage, screen and radio participating. It drew the largest gate in theatrical history—$240,520.

With doctors, nurses and hospital space limited for civilians in time of war, infantile paralysis becomes a doubly ominous threat. In the 1943 March of Dimes campaign, to swell the National Infantile Paralysis Fund, Greer Garson appeared in a film which brought before theater audiences several child victims of infantile paralysis. The next year she returned with the same children, this time on the road to health. Audiences, impressed, contributed $4,667,000 to the campaign, or 42.8 per cent of the national total. President Roosevelt voiced the Foundation's appreciation, declaring that the theaters had succeeded in interesting millions in this campaign for a charitable cause "because the motion picture is close to the lives and hearts of Americans."

The theaters also helped to overcome shortages in critical materials. Exhibitors urged patrons, especially youngsters, to "Get in the Scrap," and nearby parking lots filled up with stockpiles collected by youthful "commandos," whose admission to a movie was a piece of copper or other scrap. By the end of 1944, these theater-going salvage experts had rounded up a total of 324,000,000 pounds of rags, rubber, copper and other vital materials.

Appeals for blood donations were made in theaters, as elsewhere, to coincide with local Red Cross campaigns. Visual demonstrations on the screen prompted thousands to sign up at theater exits and make blood donations later.

Before the war, many theater managers refused to solicit funds for any cause. Theater men do not like passing the hat. It interrupts carefully timed programs, often annoys audiences who wish to relax and be entertained. When war came, both exhibitors and audiences forgot these dislikes.

The result is that the motion picture industry has helped enormously in the meeting of wartime needs. Its power to inform and influence 85,000,000 movie-goers a week was never more convincingly proved. That the industry did all this for no reward —except its self-respect and public goodwill—illustrates a hoary saying: If you want to raise money for a worthwhile cause, ask show business to help.

Movie stars of the first World War, as in this, toured America in bond selling drives. Above is the late Marie Dressler, universally beloved comedienne of another day, leading a Liberty Loan Parade in St. Louis, in 1917. Famed for her farcical "Tillie" pictures, she sold bonds, called for volunteers, sang at Army camps, spoke 14 times in one day.

Hollywood's most famous trio, Mary Pickford, Charlie Chaplin and Douglas Fairbanks, teamed up in 1918 for the Third Liberty Loan drive. Here, Charlie, brandishing his derby, perches on Doug's shoulders before New York City's Sub-Treasury building.

From the same platform Mary Pickford shouts through a megaphone to a Wall Street crowd. In those pre-microphone days stars depended upon lung power to be heard.

A quarter of a century later the same Mary (and looking much the same) sings to British troops at her Pickfair home. She has helped bond drives in both World Wars.

In a one-man bond-selling campaign in 1942, Charles Laughton stayed on the air 16 consecutive hours. He left the mike only to take orders on the telephone (above) from listeners. The bonds varied in denomination from $25 to $5,000. Total sale: $300,000.

Irving Berlin wrote two Army musical comedies; in World War I, *Yip, Yip Yaphank*, in this war, *This Is the Army*. The scene above was in both shows. *This Is the Army* toured the country, was filmed in Hollywood. Profits of over $ 7,000,000 went to Army Relief.

Symbol of the undernourished children of war-torn United Nations, Margaret O'Brien (above) played a role in the movie short, *You, John Jones,* produced for United Nations Week in 1943. Audiences contributed over $1,625,000 to the War Relief Fund.

The Hollywood Bond Cavalcade is given a big welcome home after a month's tour of the country. The crowd of 3,000 fans listens to Greer Garson as she describes the results of the trip: In sixteen major cities visited, bond sales were reported as $1,079,586,819.

Ted Gamble, of the Treasury's War Finance Division, has said: "Motion picture theaters represent 10 per cent of all physical outlets for War Bonds." Above: at one of 3,169 Bond Premières during the 4th War Loan Drive, these movie-goers buy bonds, get in free.

During the Fifth War Loan, filmdom designed, and Broadway exhibitors built, this huge cash register in New York City's Times Square. The machine weighed ten tons.

From its base, screen, stage and radio entertainers gave impromptu shows; in its drawer
were clerks and salesmen. The device helped
New York State to oversubscribe its quota.

Money was not the only thing movie audiences contributed. They gave blood as well. In picture houses all over the country the Red Cross placed workers in lobbies to sign up blood donors. In two years, more than a quarter of a million people volunteered.

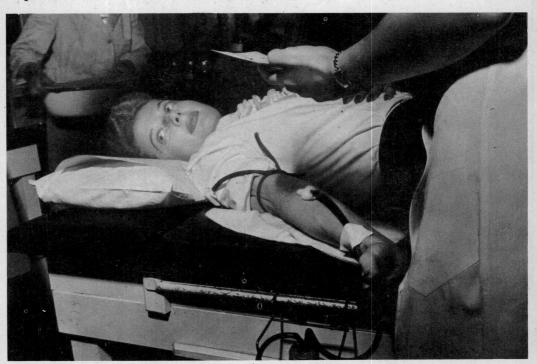

The stars gave blood, too. Here is Ann Sheridan just after her return to the U. S. from an eight-week entertainment tour of the China-Burma-India theater. When Ann landed in New York, she donated a pint of blood at the Fifth Avenue Red Cross Blood Bank.

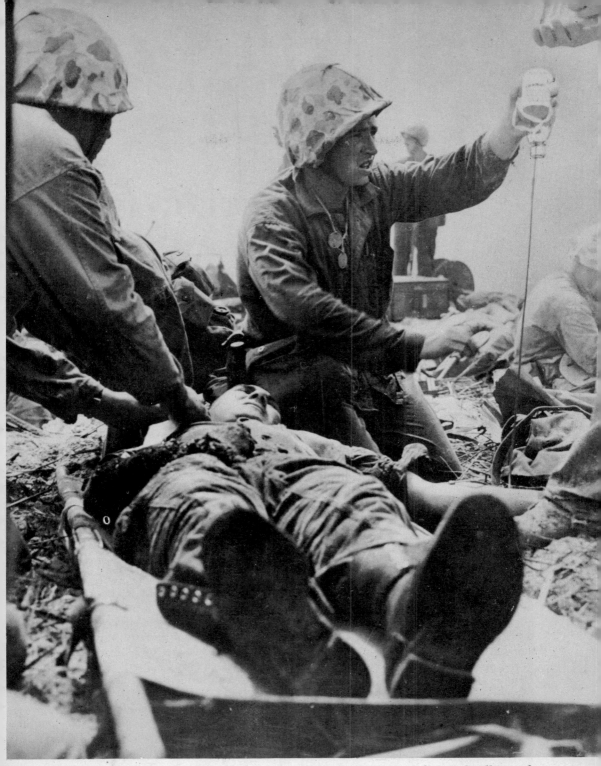

Scenes like this are taking place on every battlefront of the world. Blood plasma is used in 97 out of every 100 casualties. Thanks to the willing response of millions of American donors, many a wounded man, such as the Marine above, is alive today.

CHAPTER X

PROJECTING AMERICA

"American films are back. We have missed them sorely. Their whimsy, light touch and originality will be a welcome change after the odious Vichy-Berlin propaganda."

So wrote a Paris movie critic in September, 1944. His words were gratifying to Hollywood, but they were restrained indeed beside the reactions of other Europeans who for years had seen almost nothing but Axis propaganda films. In every country liberated by Allied arms the first civilian demand was for food; the second was usually for American movies.

This universal film hunger was generally satisfied, thanks largely to the United States Government's Office of War Information. The OWI recognized the value of American movies as a weapon of psychological warfare, arranged to distribute them abroad, augmented them heavily with screen ammunition of its own. And the Government acted none too soon.

Before the war, 75 per cent of all movie footage shown in the world was made in the United States. Hollywood stars were known all over the world, and so was Hollywood's interpretation of American life—not always a literal interpretation, to be sure, yet consistently entertaining and often informative. Hollywood was, in fact, a potent goodwill builder for America.

These facts early impressed the master propagandists in the Axis nations, who decided—and rightly—that our films were not "safe" for audiences being educated to totalitarianism. Hence American films were gradually eliminated from those markets, and homemade products were substituted. The latter were weighty with propaganda: they clarioned Fascist slogans, ridiculed the United States and democracy in general, threatened all who disagreed.

The Axis films were not notably diverting. But the dictators had ways of persuading their subjects to see them, and managed to have them shown in neutral countries. As war extended the Axis power, a major segment of the movie-going world was closed to American films.

In December, 1942, the United States Government moved to remedy this situation. In that month, the overseas branch of the OWI set up a Motion Picture Bureau to launch a counterattack on the film front. The head of the bureau was Robert Riskin, Hollywood writer-producer.

To neutral and newly liberated countries, the OWI began to send out a weekly report — called the United Newsreel — compiled from footage taken or edited by all the American newsreel companies. One purpose of these reports is to help create and maintain pro-American sentiment in neutral nations. The newsreel is likewise of obvious educational value to newly liberated peoples who have seen only highly inaccurate Axis propaganda films.

The OWI also undertook to produce and distribute abroad—in Allied, neutral, enemy-occupied and liberated countries—short, factual films of its own showing the United States and its people as they really are, so that other peoples might see us and judge for themselves.

The competition was stern. Axis studios were turning out propaganda pictures that either lied about America or were deliberately misleading. A typical trick was to piece together shots from several American newsreels and shorts to show only the bizarre side of American life—reckless driving, jitterbugging—and issue the result under some such title as *Decadent America,* or *Is This Democracy?*

One of OWI's answers was to film material from American life, using real-life people as actors, and actual places as movie lots. By the end of 1944, 52 such documentaries had been sent overseas. Twenty-eight were made by OWI under Riskin's direction, with Hollywood stars occasionally donating their services. They were supplemented by hundreds of factual shorts gathered from the armed services, from Government agencies, from industry, schools and colleges.

To sweeten and round out this diet of informational film, the OWI has distributed regular Hollywood features and short subjects abroad. These are chosen from the entire output of the studios and sound-tracked in many languages. They are pictures the OWI's Bureau itself cannot produce (one feature may cost more than the Bureau's annual budget of about $1,500,000).

For all types of pictures, the OWI has jurisdiction over details of distribution. In newly liberated areas still suffering from battle shock, movies are shown free to raise civilian morale and help military authorities secure co-operation. When order is restored and theaters are running, commercial exhibitors get the films for a standard rental fee. Money made by OWI-produced pictures is returned to the U. S. Treasury. Funds the OWI takes in for Hollywood features are put in escrow for the studios.

From the start, the OWI has worked closely with the Army's Psychological Warfare Division. The latter has handled actual distribution in enemy-occupied and just freed areas. This work has often had a quality of espionage or underground warfare. Sometimes films have been parachuted from planes to groups of patriots. Sometimes couriers have smuggled them through enemy lines—and sometimes the smugglers have been caught and killed.

When the Allied forces invaded enemy-held Europe, American films, operators and equipment went in a day or two after D-Day. Hollywood films, as well as OWI shorts, had been recorded in foreign languages several months in advance.

Pictures were shown at the first opportunity; in Sicily, for example, native audiences were watching American movies in Palermo before the island was clear of Germans. General audiences first saw the films in odd places—crowded around Army trucks, in schools, clubs, factories.

To liberated peoples, the return of American-made movies meant mass escape from war weariness. In Italy, within a few months after the Allied occupation, more people were going to movies than before the war. In France, audiences first wanted newsreels of the war, to learn what was going on in the world, and how they were personally affected by current events. Then they wanted entertainment films. Old hits like *Sergeant York* and *The Great Dictator* were new to them, and welcome.

It is self-evident that the OWI's policy of distributing moving pictures abroad in wartime has been paying dividends in goodwill for the democracies, as well as future financial dividends for Hollywood. The effect these pictures have had in counteracting Axis propaganda against America undoubtedly has been great.

The anti-Axis coalition has never boasted a clear-cut propaganda line to match the enemy's. Our "propaganda" has been the truth. We have felt that truth speaks for itself, needing only to be disseminated. In spreading truth overseas in motion pictures and other media, the OWI has done work of first importance.

According to Axis propaganda, a race riot (above), a strike, a lynching and so on occur in the United States every day. The Nazis used to get such newsreel shots from neutral sources or seize them in conquered countries, cut out footage favorable to America, weave the remainder into pictures just close enough to truth to be persuasive.

IMAGES
DE
L'AMERIQUE
Une Serie
No. 3

ELECTRIFICAREA
SATELOR

NUMMER TO
COWBOYEN

ΟΣΟΥΙΓΚΟ

LA CIUDAD
DEL ACERO

DZIPA

UMA VIAGEM

NUMMER I
SVENSKERE
I
AMERIKA

輸油管

ارتورو توسكانيني

DECACI
U
VELIKOM
GRADU

AMERIKAANSCHE
TAFEREELEN
Een Reeks
Nr. 3

One antidote to Axis screen poison has been the OWI's factual films on various aspects of American life. Here are titles from some of these pictures, indicating their extensive language coverage. Left to right, top to bottom: French, Rumanian, Norwegian, Greek, Spanish, Polish, Portuguese, Danish, Chinese, Arabic, Serbo-Croatian, Dutch.

On this and following pages are scenes from representative OWI shorts. Above: a shot from *Steel Town*, which dramatizes the people who work in American industry: The film shows foreign audiences a giant Youngstown, Ohio, steel mill; introduces the workers there and at home; presents capital and labor teamed to go all-out for victory.

Arturo Toscanini, famed Italian conductor who found haven from Fascism in America, appears in the short titled *Hymn of the Nations*. Here he leads a top-flight American symphony orchestra in music written by Verdi in the 19th century to hail Italy's fight for freedom. The film had its world première in Naples (1944), and was an instant hit.

The *Autobiography of a Jeep*, from which this scene is taken, shows in entertaining fashion how the skill and ingenuity of a nation of automobile enthusiasts were turned to the problems of mass military transportation. So successful is the film that in freed France—a nation of fashion designers—*Autobiography of a Jeep* inspired a hat style.

THE TOWN

Produced by

**THE U.S. OFFICE OF WAR INFORMATION
MOTION PICTURE BUREAU**
Overseas Branch

This OWI short was made to show other nations what America is like. The captions are based on the original sound track.

Here is a town. It lies on the banks of a quiet river. Where would you say it is?

Do you suppose that this walk leads to the shores of a blue Austrian lake?

Where do you think you can find an old Italian campanile....

Where can you find a Renaissance fountain at one end of town....

.... and where, at the other end of town, can you find a Roman temple?

Don't you know? This is an American town—created, like America itself, by men from the four corners of the earth.

Johnny McGuire, shown here in his office, works on the town's newspaper. His grandfather came from Ireland.

Mr. Wunderlich arrived from Germany over half a century ago. But his friend, Mrs. Antel, was born here.

This farmer, Mr. Feidir, stands by a scale as his forefathers stood in a market square in Central Europe.

The Datillo family have been in the United States all their lives. But they still like Italian food.

The name of their town is Madison. It lies on the Ohio River in the state of Indiana. It was named for a President.

Like thousands of similar communities, Madison draws its life from the fields and farms that surround it.

This part of Indiana, like many other parts of the United States, is very good for dairy farming. . . .

. . . . and vegetable-growing. Here, as in many other lands, Saturday is market day. And the farm trucks roll in . . .

. . . to Main Street, heart of every American town—yet part of a highway that spans a continent. There's room here!

At night, the bowling alley is highly popular with the farmers and with the townspeople, men and women both.

One meeting-place in any American town is the corner drugstore . . .

... though some folks like to gather for a quiet glass of beer ...

... and the young people, here as everywhere, enjoy their dancing ...

... while, in the school auditorium, the orchestra gives its Saturday concert.

Sunday is set aside as a day of rest and a day for worship.

The people who came from all over the world brought their churches with them.

All faiths have found a place here. No one interferes with another's freedom to worship when and where he pleases.

Monday, in this as in other parts of the country, means work again . . .

. . . and school, free—and compulsory—to all the children of the community. Each has equal opportunity to learn.

The children study the history of man's struggle to govern himself: Magna Charta, the Declaration of Independence . . .

. . . and they are taught other languages, to equip them to become better citizens of the world.

In towns like this, a great part of the community budget is devoted to the children—the coming generation.

The games children play here may not be the same as in every other land. But the spirit of childhood is universal.

This is the mayor of the town. The people hire him and the people can fire him. He's their servant—and proud of it.

If any trouble arises in this town, it is settled in the presence of the people, at a trial held in public.

The judge is elected by the people. So is the public prosecutor.

The people cast their votes as they see fit. In free countries, the only thing secret about government is the ballot.

These are the people. To the banks of a New World river their fathers brought the culture and heritage of the Old.

Now their sons have gone back, to join the fight for freedom—to make this town and all towns free and secure forever.

CHAPTER XI

HOLLYWOOD IS JUST

ANOTHER TOWN AT WAR

The day after Pearl Harbor, Hollywood became a military camp. Within 24 hours, 100 studio trucks and drivers were transporting Army troops and equipment; studio arsenals were being stripped of prop rifles, revolvers, machine guns and ammunition to fortify undersupplied posts along the coast. Studios mobilized their fire-fighting equipment. The beach in front of Hollywood's spacious homes at Malibu soon swarmed with soldiers moved from inland training camps. The West Coast felt that there was danger of an immediate Japanese attack.

Studio buildings were camouflaged; black-out regulations were enforced; air raid shelters, complete with hospital units, were built on studio lots.

In personal terms, the war was brought home shockingly to the film colony when, early in 1942, the plane carrying Carole Lombard from an Indianapolis War Bond Rally crashed and burned. It was like a small town learning that one of its most popular young men had fallen on Bataan.

Hollywood had been growing into a war town long before Pearl Harbor, and the conversion was soon complete. Near-by Army and Navy camps swelled in numbers and size. Defense plants expanded. Trains, buses, cars rolled in bringing troops and war workers. And Hollywood's problems became—and as the year 1945 opened they remained—those of other war towns: transportation, housing, feeding, relaxation.

Members of the film colony flocked into various war organizations: Red Cross, Naval Aid Auxiliary, Canteen Services, the American Women's Voluntary Services, Army Camps Emergency Services. Membership in these groups increased in each war year.

Scarcely a branch of film production remained unaffected by the war. Travel restrictions imposed by Washington discouraged the use of distant locations. No cameras were allowed near Army reservations, dams, or war plants. Sea shots were forbidden in harbors from San Diego to Seattle. Train shots were impossible — the armed forces had requisitioned all available rolling stock. Black-out regulations eliminated night shooting.

As the war continued such restrictions were gradually relaxed. But meanwhile the industry had learned valuable lessons — in economy, for one thing.

Hollywood was profligate in its spending before the war. But it quickly became a miser when lavish sets were ruled out for the duration to save money and materials.

Its artisans of make-believe outdid even their own miracle-working selves. Wood took the place of masonry and concrete. When a fire scene was shot, an asbestos screen was painted to look like wood. Hidden gas jets were ignited and the cameras caught a realistic shot of a burning house—with no materials damaged. Sets were constructed that could be adapted to multiple uses. Their framework was permanent, but windows, doors, fireplaces, etc., were removable. By ingenious alterations a night club could be made to look like a hotel lobby, an airport, a railroad station. Studios swapped expensive movable sets, replicas of ships, for example.

To offset the critical nail shortage an enterprising technician invented a device like a carpet sweeper (now used in most studios) which picked up stray nails, to be sorted and straightened. Hardware fixtures were replaced with glass or plastics. Hairpins—studios were limited to two pounds a month—were checked in and out of dressing rooms as if they were gems. They were used, sterilized, and used again. When Chinese imports were cut off, make-up men stopped making wigs of human hair. Camel's hair brushes for applying make-up were sent to aircraft plants for dusting precision instruments. Cops-and-robbers pursuit scenes, in which autos full of gasoline raced around curves with screeching but beautiful new tires, were dim memories.

Hollywood has drastically limited its raw film consumption. Directors are instructed to rehearse scenes thoroughly before turning the camera; actors are advised to come on the set with lines well memorized.

As the war progressed, more defense workers, more servicemen poured into an already overburdened town. By the end of 1944, it seemed as if every serviceman in southern California with a 48-hour pass descended on the film capital.

Like all U. S. towns, Hollywood welcomed its uniformed visitors, crowded though it was. Studios, which had closed their doors to all tourists, opened them to men with overseas records, conducted them around the lots, let them meet their favorite stars.

On many of the sets war films were being produced and servicemen stood by, fascinated, as they watched the make-believe scenes they had lived through in reality. It was not unheard of for a soldier, strolling between lots, to snap to attention and salute some extra costumed in the uniform of a three-star general.

On week ends servicemen outnumbered civilians ten to one on the streets of downtown Hollywood. At first, they had to sleep in parks and in theaters which offered their aisles and lobbies. Then Hollywood unlocked its doors. High schools set up dormitories. Private homes welcomed men on furlough. California's theaters collected $190,000 from audiences in a "Bed for Buddies" campaign. (The sum matched the amount contributed by the State for the same purpose.) Anne Lehr's Guild took care of thousands of stranded visitors.

"Ma" Lehr, as she is known to countless uniformed youngsters, is a stout, motherly-looking woman who has devoted her life to charity. Her Guild, for impoverished screen folk, became the Hollywood Guild and Canteen shortly after Pearl Harbor. Starting with sleeping accommodations for 35 men, it soon had 1,000 beds. One section is reserved for officers, another for WAVES, WACs, SPARS and Women Marines. The building has a pool and a gigantic ice box with raiding privileges.

In addition to the innumerable USO's which dot the town, Hollywood can also be proud of its famous Canteen—not to be confused with Anne Lehr's Guild and Canteen. The huge building was designed by studio art directors. Studio painters, electricians, carpenters worked on it after hours and without pay. A "name" band plays there every night and servicemen dance with Hedy Lamarr, Betty Grable, Olivia de Havilland—sometimes with the Canteen's president, Bette Davis. Between dances, stars appear on the stage in impromptu acts. Such bus boys as Walter Pidgeon, Spencer Tracy and Humphrey Bogart wash dishes.

During the war Hollywood has not contented itself with dispensing its most noted product—glamour. It has given in addition what other American towns have given—labor and money, blood and lives. Now it awaits the day when its sons return to parade up Hollywood Boulevard.

Meanwhile, Hollywood is just another town at war.

This is a daytime view of Hollywood Boulevard. With tires and gas rationed, auto traffic, as in many other U. S. towns, has been cut to a quarter of its pre-war volume.

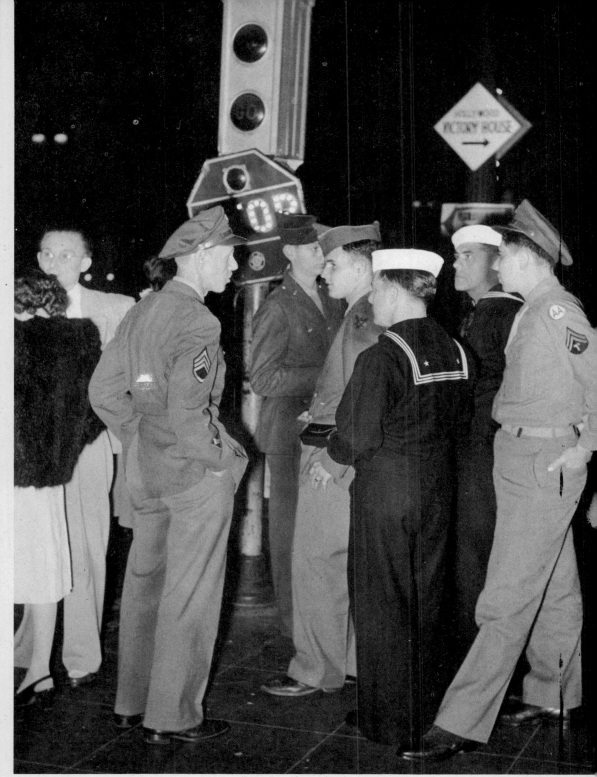

The streets of the film capital are always crowded with servicemen. Above is the famous corner, "Hollywood and Vine," where visiting servicemen gather at all hours.

"Help wanted" signs like this soon dotted Hollywood's streets as the war got under way. In 1944 war workers outnumbered movie makers by far more than ten to one.

With the influx of defense workers Hollywood became an all night town. Amusement places knew no hours. Above: a crowd waits to see the 3 A.M. showing of a feature film.

In 1943, 41 per cent of all movies had a war background of one sort or another. Here, a studio make-up expert fits actor Robert Watson for his role in an anti-Nazi picture.

Hollywood glamour is used to show home owners what to do in the event of a Jap air raid. Above: beruffled starlets demonstrate how to quench a fire with a stirrup pump.

As in all American towns, Hollywood's Roll of Honor is a source of pride to citizens. This is Hollywood's record: 6,000 men in uniform out of the town's 30,000 film makers.

A photograph of Betty Grable is used to instruct soldiers in map reading. The grinning veteran says it's easy to keep one's mind on the map when Betty is the background.

On the lighter side of Hollywood's war effort are its world-famous beauties who pose for pin-up pictures. The photographs are heartily esteemed by servicemen, as the

walls of barracks and ships' bulkheads show. Above: Lucille Ball before the mirror, doubling the delightful view. On the left: Miss Ball's image. On the right: Miss Ball.

Theater lobbies like this are no longer seen in Hollywood. Movie audiences generously supported a "Bed For Buddies" drive, thus helped find lodgings for men on furlough.

One famed Hollywood haven for service-men and women is Anne Lehr's Canteen. Here they can eat, dance, get a bed for the night, and, just as important, write "Mom."

At the Hollywood Canteen, where 700 host-
esses are on the list, a band plays nightly
for dancing. Here, Martha O'Driscoll cuts
a rug with a fortunate private first class.

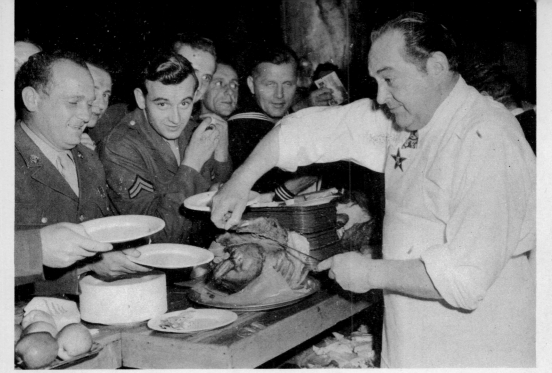

Between dances servicemen storm the free lunch counter where they are served by stars acting in the roles of waiters. Affable Edward Arnold (above) deftly slices a ham.

On a visit to San Diego's Naval Training Station, Jane Russell (sighting gun) and Cita Raymond (in background) relax at a nearby amusement park with a naval convoy.

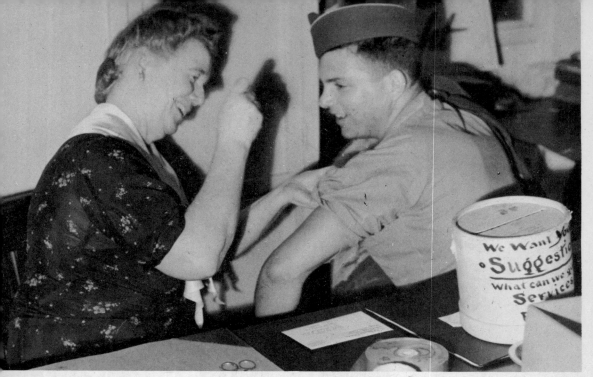

Guests of "Ma" Lehr's Guild and Canteen can raid the icebox at any hour, do their own washing, or like this soldier, have a quick repair job done with thread and needle.

A Canteen bulletin board records a variety of messages in chalk: "Al . . . call Western Union;" "Chas. meet us at the Palladium, same table;" "For sale, black shoes, 10½C."

Real life scenes are played at Los Angeles' Union Station. The crowd looks on joyfully as this gunner's mate, oblivious of spectators, gets a colossal Hollywood embrace.

CHAPTER XII

EPILOGUE TO WAR

Preceding chapters have shown what motion pictures and the motion picture industry have contributed to the war. Both will face an even greater challenge and opportunity with the coming of peace.

Heretofore the motion picture has been primarily a medium of entertainment—one of the most popular ever devised. Post-war Hollywood will still make boy-meets-girl romances, decorative musicals, light-hearted comedies. Hollywood did not throw away its golden slippers when it put on G.I. boots.

Entertainment films doubtless will be more popular than ever as world markets are reopened, and improved techniques increase the screen's appeal and effectiveness. Vast strides have been made in the use of color, for example. Sound and animation have shown similar progress.

If the motion picture is to fulfill all its potentialities, however, to a degree never before imagined it must purvey not only entertainment but information.

A trend in this direction had started even before Pearl Harbor—as long ago as the 1927 advent of sound to the screen. Newsreels and serious shorts illustrate this. The war has vastly accelerated the trend.

The war has provided filmdom with an enormous laboratory in which the efficacy of motion pictures in teaching, training, and imparting information generally has been conclusively proved. It has developed a huge backlog of personnel—photographers, directors, technicians—experienced in all phases of movie-making and enthusiastic about the screen's potentialities. And it has brought about improvement and standardization of the essential mechanism for showing film under all kinds of conditions, from steaming jungle to vibrating ship deck—the 16-mm. film projector.

Both 16-mm. camera and 16-mm. projector have some advantages over standard equipment (35-mm.), to compensate for some disadvantages. They are far less expensive, easier to transport. Film in 16-mm. size is safer to handle and to store since it is made of slow-burning acetate, whereas the 35-mm. is of explosive nitrate.

Before the war thousands of 16-mm. projectors could show only silent film, and those made for sound film ran the scale from museum pieces to latest models. The needs of the armed services were so pressing that all manufacturers expanded production, incorporated last minute improvements and developed a sturdy, standardized portable case. It is uncertain how many of the projectors which have gone to war will return in usable shape. But manufacturers are already planning to turn out quantities of tested equipment for various civilian uses as soon as labor and materials can be obtained.

Even today, in the United States, millions of feet of film are shown that the average movie fan never sees. Much of it, made by independent producers in the larger cities, is unseen by Hollywood. Its sources are as varied as its subjects. A department store uses the screen to show its saleswomen how to serve customers; a museum offers a short to high school classes on camouflage in nature; a religious group puts out a film for its member churches.

When peace comes, use of 16-mm. film by schools, churches and other institutions undoubtedly will expand. It is even possible that 16-mm. film will develop its own commercial theaters. This market will beckon the makers of entertainment, industrial and educational pictures, in and out of Hollywood, who expect to produce films for 16-mm. projection.

In the post-war world, informational films are expected to find important uses in the following fields, among others:

International Understanding: The Allied governments have already demonstrated the value of motion pictures in interpreting one nation's way of life to others.

Several of these governments have film units corresponding to those in the U. S. Office of War Information and the Co-ordinator of Inter-American Affairs. At the beginning of 1945, the CIAA had sent nearly 400 informational films to South America.

The United Nations Relief and Rehabilitation Administration plans to use films made by the Allied governments among peoples in areas liberated from the Axis.

Rehabilitation of Veterans: Films will aid the returning serviceman (or woman) to readjust to civilian living. One noteworthy Army picture, *Meet McGonigle*, depicts a veteran of the first World War who, despite the loss of both hands, quickly learned to resume his former way of life. By showing that McGonigle shaves, dresses, eats, types, drives, shoots pool, even flies an airplane without help from others, the film infuses amputation cases of this war with new life, hope, and self-respect.

Community Problems: As peace brings home-front problems—prevention of juvenile delinquency, resettlement of war-uprooted populations, improved housing—16-mm. films can help to keep the public informed. In recent years, both 35-mm. documentaries and entertainment films (e.g., *Youth In Crisis, Are These Our Children?*) have dealt with such subjects, but possibilities in the field barely have been scratched.

Religion: The attitude of religious leaders toward motion pictures has lately been revolutionized. Keenly aware of the necessity of holding the interest of movie-going members, many church groups intend after the war to supplement religious instruction with inspirational and educational films.

Industry: American business has been one of the largest users of 16-mm. films, chiefly to tell its story (how tires are made, how coal is mined) to schools, civic organizations and other groups of potential customers.

Industry—often in cooperation with the Government—also has used films to train new workers or teach old ones new skills. When peace and reconversion come, there may be a boom in films to teach war-born changes in manufacturing methods.

Science and Medicine: A specialized value of motion pictures is their ability to make scientific and medical discoveries quickly available to teachers and students. After the war, 16-mm. may be widely used to spread knowledge of medical techniques (see Part 2 of this chapter).

Education: This war has shown servicemen how ably films can act as teachers. As students and instructors, now in uniform, return to civilian life, probably they will be eager to use motion pictures in the classroom. Meanwhile other educators are also realizing what films can do. Many modern schools have facilities for motion picture projection. Education is clearly a field in which 16-mm. pictures have a future (see Part 3 of this chapter).

Democracy: As part of its job as educator, the film must help to preserve and inculcate, at home and abroad, belief in democratic principles and institutions (see Part 4 of this chapter).

Succeeding pages illustrate a few of the uses to which films will be put in the post-war world. They can help enormously to make it the One World of which men dream.

International understanding may be based on small, human things—such as a picture of a child in a war-torn area gnawing the only available food. This picture is from the Canadian-made film, *In the Wake of the Armies,* which is distributed by the UNRRA.

Understanding also stems from knowledge of other people's cultural progress. Movies providing such information can help to fur- ther international cooperation. Above: students at the University of Moscow. Russia will see similar films of the American life.

Prominent among America's current domestic problems is that of returning war veterans. Here a discharged soldier applies for work in a factory. Just as motion pictures helped train him to fight, so can they benefit him later in the post-war industrial world.

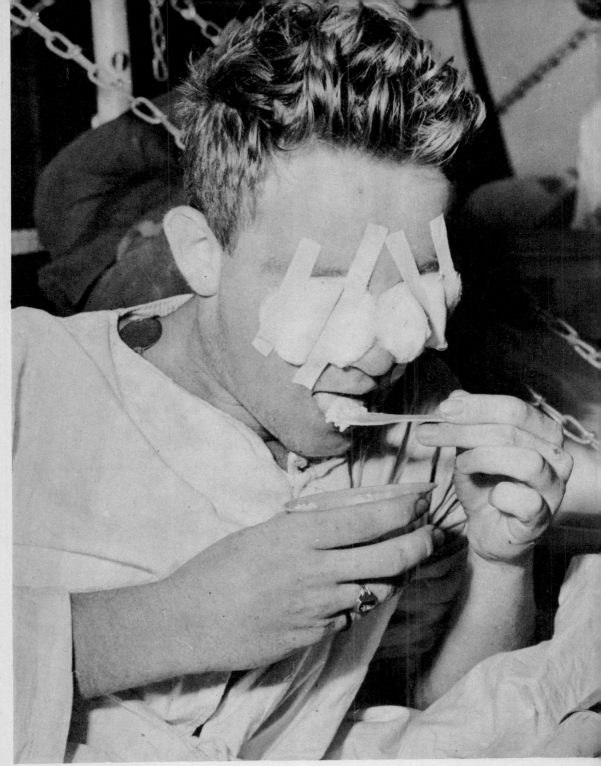

Demobilization of our multi-million army is complicated by the special problem of the physically or mentally disabled. Films will benefit even the blind, by instructing those who care for them professionally and those who will eventually greet them at home.

In the field of sociology, the informational film has a notable opportunity to show conditions demanding aroused civic action. Example: the neglected child above, calmly puffing a cigarette. He appears in the 16-mm. documentary short, *And So They Live*.

Another subject for civic concern is town planning, particularly in the post-war period. Films can help point the way; already a remarkable visualization exists in *The City*, which contrasts crowded slum conditions with properly planned housing (above).

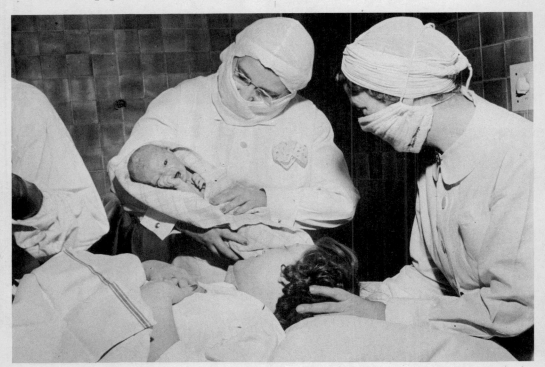

The next generation can be a better generation if people are shown means of making it so. *Child Care*, distributed by the U. S. Office of Education, offers instruction from birth of the child (above) through adolescence. More films like this are clearly needed.

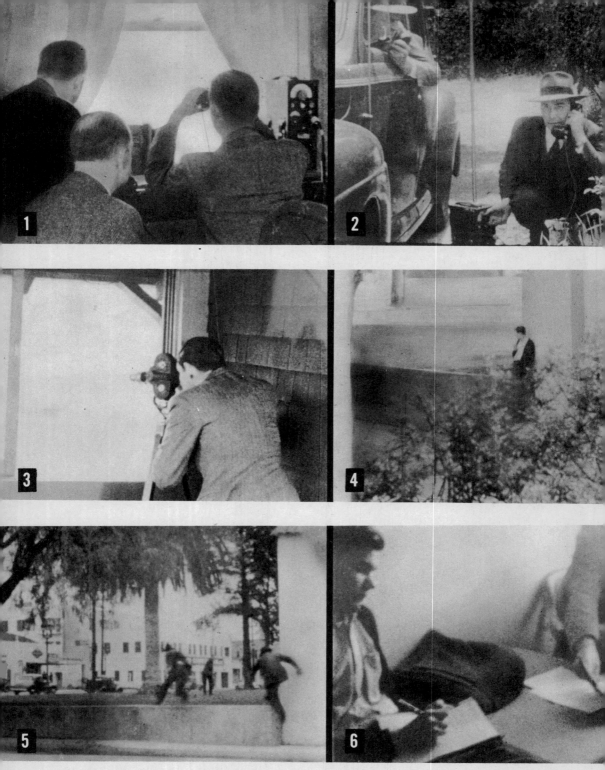

Crime detection will profit from use of films. This FBI sequence records the Betty Grable extortion case. FBI agents watch the payoff scene (1), communicate via walkie-talkie (2), photograph the extortioner (3), chase him (4, 5) and obtain his confession (6).

First used by church mission boards to visualize the needs in foreign fields for those at home, religious films, as well as educational shorts, are now popular with church groups. The Religious Film Association lists about 200 films as suitable for church work.

In industry, vocational training is being speeded by motion pictures; workers learn faster, retain better when taught by vocational films. Above: a picture on one phase of steel making. The Office of Education has produced over 150 training pictures.

Agriculture can also benefit from films. This picture shows a tractor-drawn damming lister, developed for semi-arid and dry farm-ing. This is not an extract from a movie, but in the post-war world informational films can have fully as much picture impact.

Two ways in which 16-mm. film can be used by American business appear on this page. Above: window decorators show how their craft is practiced. Post-war business will make good use of movies to train personnel in the most efficient means of performing jobs.

This is a still photograph of an oil company's cracking plant. After the war, movie shots of industrial plants and processes will be used more and more. They are accurate, can be highly entertaining, and are valuable in advertising and public relations work.

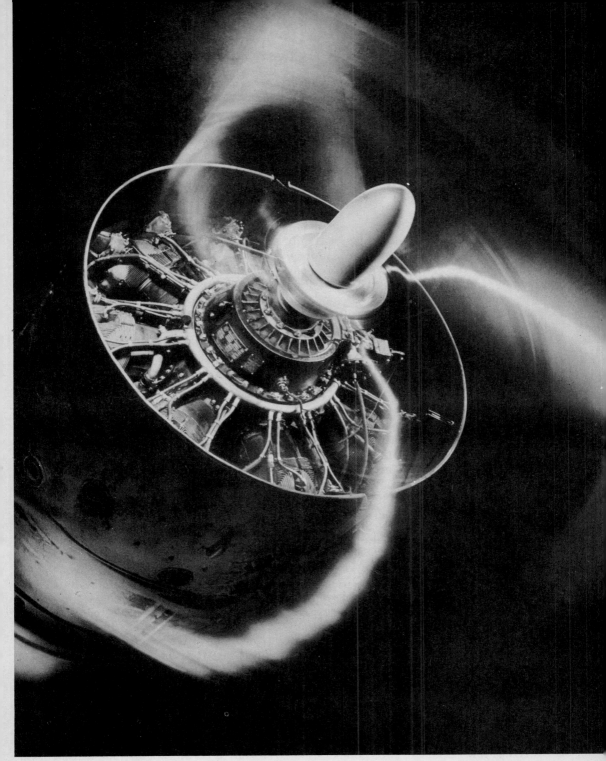

Industrial research finds a special use for moving pictures: slow motion can follow action too fast for the eye. Above: a Wright Cyclone engine moves at 2,400 revolutions a minute. Thanks to film, visual powers of tomorrow's engineers will be increased.

Part 2: FILMS FOR HEALTH

Of the men classified 4-F by Selective Service in this war, nearly half carried the scars of malnutrition. Of the first two million selectees examined by the Army, 48 of every 1,000 were rejected for syphilis. Two million Americans suffer from intermittent malaria. We have 750,000 victims of mental and nervous disorders in institutions. Tuberculosis afflicts up to three of every 100 American war workers.

These are facts to disturb any thinking person. Science and medicine have advanced tremendously in the last century—what of the future? Can this country conquer the blight of disease that still hangs over much of our population? Can other countries, technically less advanced than we, move forward with us to a world less afflicted by physical and mental ills?

The answer lies, at least in some small degree, in motion pictures. No matter what progress scientists and technicians may make, their work will be of comparatively little value if it is not widely disseminated. The 16-mm. film can help to disseminate it.

In the war against disease, movies are a weapon dating back to 1900; medical films were among the first ever made. But we are only starting to use that weapon. So far these films have taken two main forms: non-technical pictures, to teach laymen good health practices, and medical pictures, usually highly technical, to record and analyze the work of doctors and surgeons for other professionals, including students.

Hundreds of health films have been made, and exhibited to hundreds of thousands of people. But their impact, according to Dr. Adolf Nichtenhauser of the American Film Center, has been relatively small. They often have lacked quality, often have been ill-suited for their audiences. Too rarely have they been made for those who need them most: the uneducated and underprivileged, whose health and sanitation standards are low because of ignorance and poverty.

Yet some fine health films have been produced. A few years ago, Pare Lorentz's *The Fight for Life* attracted wide attention. This tells of the underprivileged mothers at Chicago's Maternity Center; its climax is an actual delivery, in which a young intern saves the lives of both mother and child. *Before the Doctor Comes*, based on the Red Cross first-aid textbook, had a broad distribution early in the war. *Life Begins* records the work of the Yale Clinic of Child Development—a complete story of babyhood. *Health Is a Victory*, made and distributed by the U. S. Office of Education, offers a frank discussion of gonorrhea.

Probably the most effective health films to date are those produced by Walt Disney for distribution to Latin America. Sample titles: *Water, Friend or Enemy* (on water pollution); *The Human Body; Winged Scourge* (on malaria). This last film has been shown thousands of times to audiences aggregating millions. To many Central and South Americans, Disney is Uncle Sam.

In the post-war world there obviously will be a need for further expansion in health films. Meanwhile a parallel demand exists for rapid dissemination of new medical and surgical discoveries among medical men. Here again the 16-mm. picture can be of great service.

Up to now, almost every field of operative surgery has been covered by the moving-picture camera, but the coverage has often been incomplete, technically inadequate.

Now tremendous possibilities exist for the use of film in teaching both medical and surgical techniques. Training in diagnosis and care can be greatly speeded: one picture can cover, in a few minutes, the whole span of a disease from symptom recognition through treatment and results. Surgical techniques can be shown via film to thousands of doctors instead of to a mere handful jammed into an operating amphitheater.

Such films have been made; more will be. Drs. Ernst Herz and Tracy Putnam of New York are among those experimenting in the field (see pages 260, 261). One surgical picture on eye muscles explains the technique in terms of animation. Discoveries in the subject of psychiatry also are being filmed.

A nation prospers as the well-being of its citizens is advanced. In that truism lies a challenge to the makers and distributors of 16-mm. motion pictures.

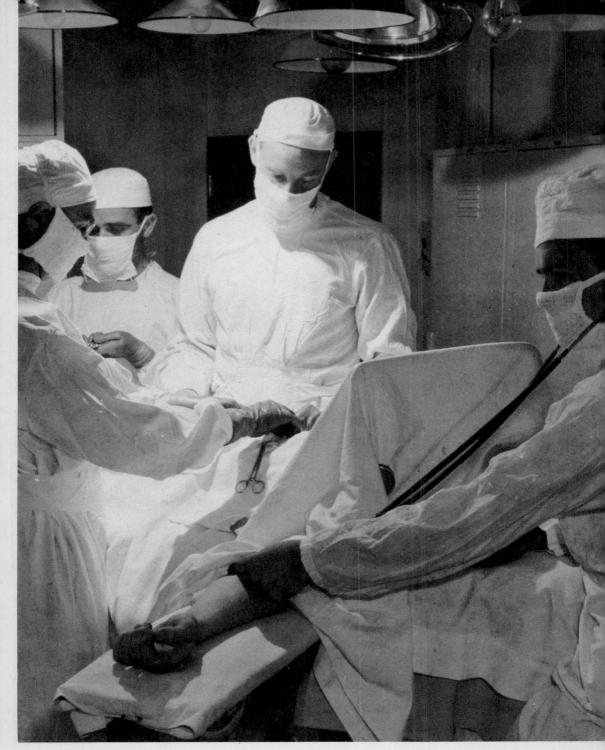

The skill of a trained surgeon can avert disease, remedy disability, save life. But one man, however able, cannot succor humanity single-handed. Here is a field for motion pictures: transmitting techniques developed by the brilliant few to the eager many. For an example of a film explaining a specific surgical operation, turn the page.

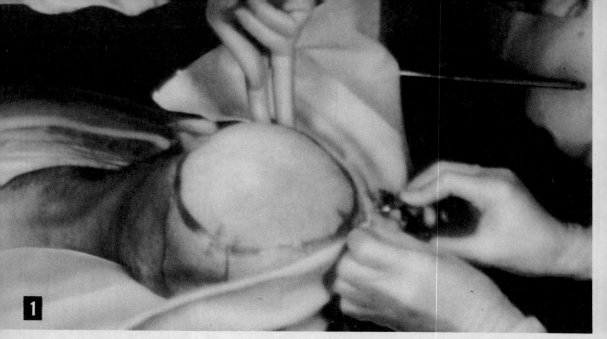

The preliminary steps of the brain operation shown here were filmed by Dr. Ernst Herz, at the Neurological Institute of Columbia Medical Center, in New York. Above, drapes are being pinned in place close to the line of incision already marked by the surgeon on the patient's shaved head. A local anesthetic has been infiltrated along the incision line.

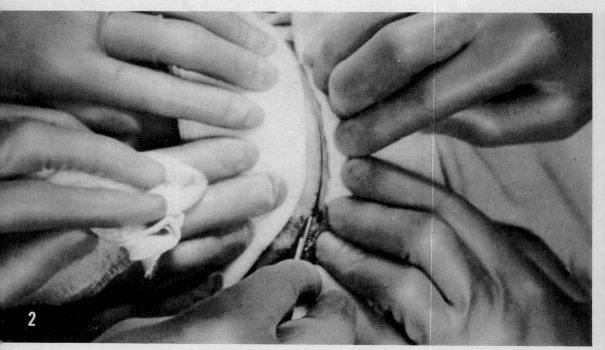

All but a small section of the indicated line is incised, with the scalp tamponed against the skull by firm finger pressure as the cut is made. Even slight relaxation of this pressure allows serious bleeding. Numerous long clamps, seen in the following pictures, are later applied to the severed blood vessels along both sides of the line of incision.

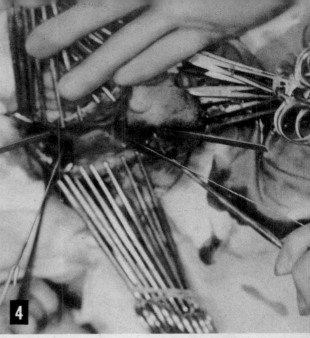

Next stage: four or five holes are then carefully drilled through the skull. As the picture shows, skin and soft tissue are held back by fork-like instruments called retractors.

A saw guide (ends at lower left and right) is run through one hole and out the next, to protect brain from saw. Saw is inserted on the guide; handles are attached to the ends.

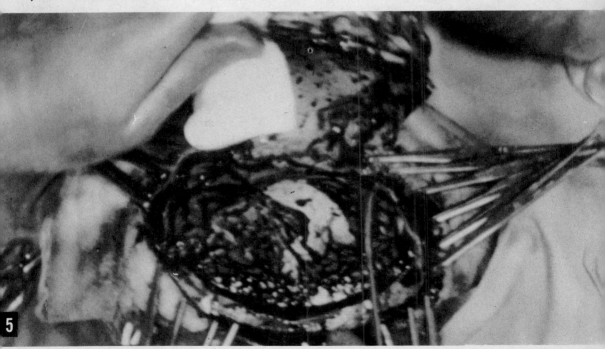

After the first bone bridge is sawed through, the process is repeated until all the sections are cut except the small one under the unincised skin area. The bone flap is then broken up and the whole section lifted. The main operation on the brain itself is now ready to begin, about half an hour after the first step pictured here was started.

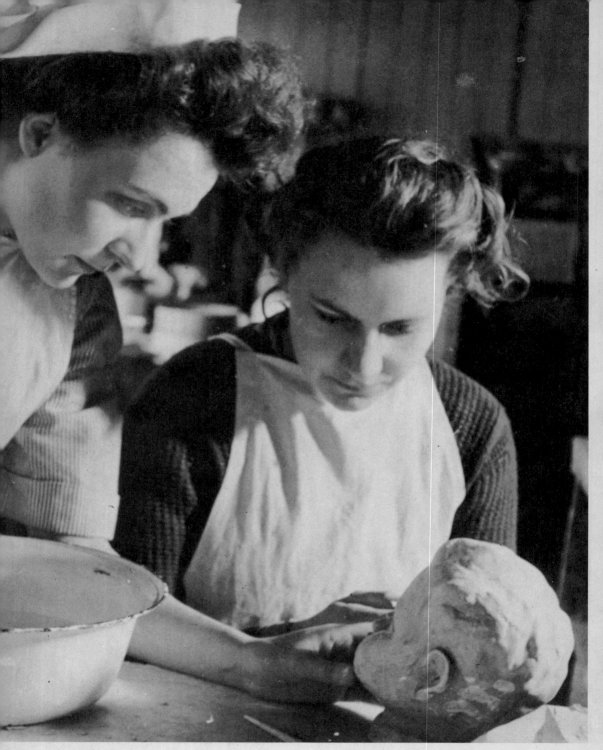

Psychiatry, the study and treatment of damaged minds, also can be demonstrated on film. This scene is from a noteworthy effort in the field, the British-made *Psychiatry in Action*. It shows a sufferer from war neurosis modeling a child's head in clay—one of many types of therapy now used to aid patients suffering from mental disturbance.

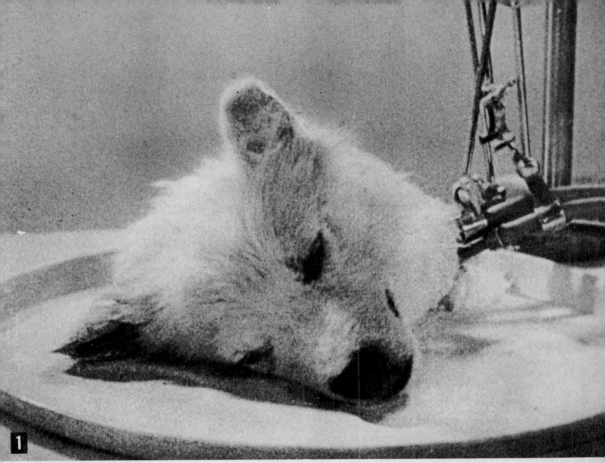

1

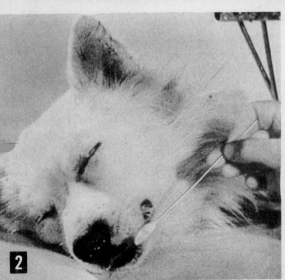

2

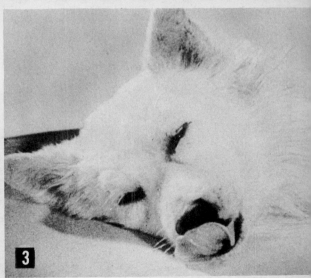

3

Here is a demonstration of a different order —a sequence from a startling Russian picture on an experiment with the head of a dead dog. Top: ten minutes after heart action and breathing stop, circulation is restored by an autoinjector. Left: citric acid is applied to dog's lip. Right: dog licks his lip—apparent evidence of life revived.

EL ENEMIGO UNVISIBLE

The Unseen Enemy, a Walt Disney health film, warns Latin Americans against microbes. Captions are based on narration.

You've learned to grow fine crops, to raise pigs and chickens. These things all protect you from the enemy—hunger.

And if a storm comes you find shelter in your house, for you've learned to protect yourself from the weather, too.

But even a house won't protect you from your worst enemy . . . a great unseen enemy, deadly and silent.

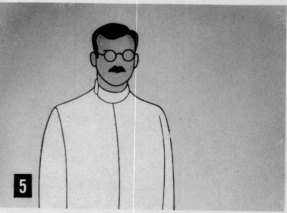

No, no! Wait! It's no use running away. Disease can be anywhere. No one can run away from . . . disease!

Let's call on a man who knows all about it—the doctor. He studies disease every day, using a wonderful instrument.

6 Doctor, we'll borrow your glasses. The instrument the doctor uses makes things look bigger than they are.

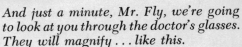

7 And just a minute, Mr. Fly, we're going to look at you through the doctor's glasses. They will magnify . . . like this.

8 But let's try a stronger magnifying glass. You see, now the fly looks a great deal bigger than it really is.

9 If we use a still stronger glass he begins to look like a monster. Look at his leg! It's covered with hair.

10 Now if we take four glasses and put a tube around them we have a microscope. By looking through this instrument we

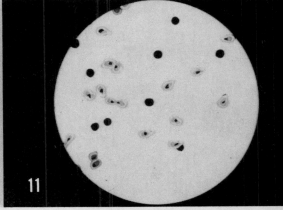

11 . . . can see the tiny creatures that cause disease. This piece of glass has a drop of water on it, full of germs.

265

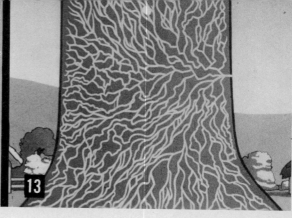

See this little beetle boring a hole in the tree? One tiny beetle certainly can't hurt a big tree like this.

Look! The beetle's drilled deep into the wood and laid its eggs. Finally there are thousands, eating away at the tree.

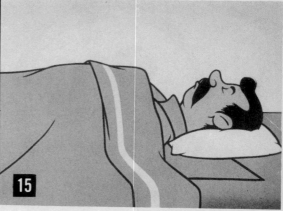

And that's the way these tiny germs attack a big strong body like yours. For that's what happens when you drink bad water.

At first there may be only a few germs. As they grow fat they multiply like the beetles and soon you are a very sick man.

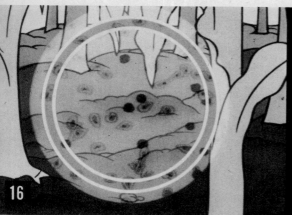
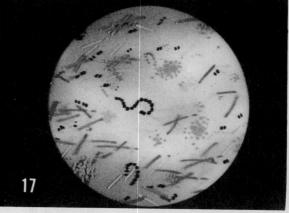

It isn't only in the water that we find these little killers. Suppose we take a look around your farm.

You see! Here they are! The vicious, deadly killers that live in the soil fouled with human waste.

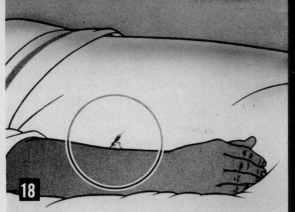

18

19

Now, let's go inside your house. This mosquito carries germs inside his body and when he bites he'll leave germs in you.

And how about the flies in your house? They leave thousands of germs behind as they drag their legs across your table.

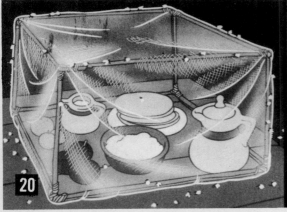

20

21

The flies seem harmless enough but they carry all kinds of dirt and filth. So cover your food so the flies can't get at it: . . .

And cover your bed at night; then the mosquitoes can't reach you and you'll be safe from the disease they carry.

22

23

The germs we saw in the water can be killed. They can be killed by boiling water before you drink it.

Protect yourself from disease wherever you find it and you will make your life healthy, happy and prosperous.

Part 3: FILMS FOR THE CLASSROOM

Both for adult education and for the training of youth of all ages, the motion picture holds rich promise. Efforts to use films in the classroom have been made for years. But teachers were not trained to use them, projectors were not widely available, and suitable films were often non-existent or at least hard to obtain.

War has broken these bottlenecks.

Teachers and students in the services are learning the how and why of informational films; projectors will be plentiful at the war's end; good informational films, some made during the war with private funds, but most with government funds, will be readily available for general use. In subject matter they will range all the way from a film on the proper use of the screw driver (simple mechanics) to films on the birth of the snapping turtle (zoology), the structure of the earth (geology), or even a film on language instruction—for example, Basic English (philology).

Meanwhile, an increasing number of educational films is being made and distributed by endowed institutions, by commercial firms, and by universities and state departments of education—Ohio's, serving 1600 communities, distributes more films than all the commercial exchanges in the state. Other makers or distributors of educational films include Teaching Films Custodians, Inc., the Universities of California, Georgia and Indiana, the American Museum of Natural History, and the Y.M.C.A. Motion Picture Bureau, with four exchanges.

A leader in the field is Encyclopedia Britannica Films, sponsored by the University of Chicago, which has a library of more than 500 films designed for use in high school and college. Typical subjects are: *Work of Volcanoes, The Earth's Rocky Crust,* for geology students; *Electrons,* and *Theory of Flight,* for physics classes. Results are often striking —a university which used to spend two and a half weeks teaching the molecular theory now, with the aid of the screen, covers it in two and a half days.

Educators know that the film should be used as an adjunct to other teaching methods, not as a substitute for them. Encyclopedia Britannica makes constant surveys of school text books and curricula and works closely with teachers to fit its films to classroom needs.

The University of Chicago is also planning a study center where all kinds of visual materials, including motion pictures and slide films, will be collected for the use of researchers and students in this field.

A five-year study to determine the need for educational films and set up standards for them has been launched by a commission of the American Council of Education, which is financed by the picture industry.

Walt Disney describes the goal when he says: "We must work to train the coming generation so that no schoolroom can be so small or so remote that it shall lack the benefits of educational film."

One specialized branch of the educational film is the Human Relations Series compiled by Alice V. Keliher, professor of education at New York University.

Each of these films consists of sequences of pictures concerning human behavior excerpted from Hollywood commercial features. They are designed to stimulate classroom discussion.

"Possibly the most important thing we can do with these films," says Dr. Keliher, "is to extend students' awareness of the many, many ways people live their lives. All of us suffer from the limitations of our own experience . . . We suspect the different. We are intolerant of it because we fear it. If we are to reduce fear and thereby get human beings to lower their defenses in favor of a positive group life, we must bring man out of the realm of the unknown."

Problem situations are selected from feature pictures—theft of money, prideful lying, exploitation of labor—and students are invited to discuss them.

On the following pages are excerpts from typical human relations films—the French film *La Maternelle,* which depicts the suffering of an abandoned child hungry for security which a responsive adult can offer, and *Fury,* which reveals the speed with which gossip can spread through a town and culminate in the murder of an innocent man.

Excerpt from *La Maternelle,* French-made film, tells the story of neglected six-year-old Marie. Left in a day nursery, she becomes attached to a maid, Rose (foreground).

Rose takes Marie to the house where her mother, a prostitute, lives. The landlady (right) says there is no one to care for the child. Rose takes Marie to her own home.

Rose's love for Marie wins the heart of the nursery doctor, who proposes and is accepted. As Marie watches the happy couple, she feels forgotten and shut out from love.

Rose leaves with the doctor to look at their future home. Marie thinks that Rose has deserted her, as her own mother did. She wanders to the docks to drown herself.

Marie is rescued and brought back to the nursery. Now Rose realizes how much Marie needs her love. She decides Marie must stay with her and the doctor when·they marry.

"FURY"

Another human relations picture is *Fury*, starring Spencer Tracy. As Joe Wilkinson (above), he reads about a recent kidnapping. Joe is innocent of the crime . . .

. . . but he is picked up on the road and brought in for questioning by the county sheriff. The evidence against him is purely circumstantial, but Joe is held on suspicion.

The sheriff's deputy tells a barroom crowd that a suspect has been arrested. At this point the students are able to watch the formation of a chain of vicious gossip...

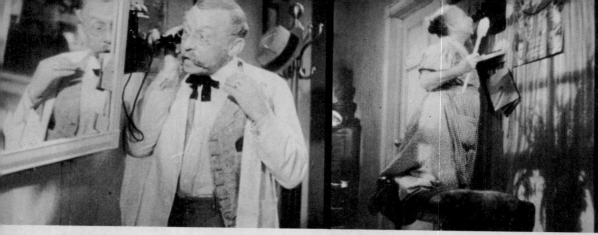

In quick, dramatic scenes the rumors spread . . . The town barber telephones his wife.

The barber's wife raps on the window to attract the attention of the next door neighbor.

Eager for gossip, the neighbor leans from her window, listens intently to the story.

Next person to hear the story, now beyond control, is a woman on her way to market.

At the market, the woman tells the rumor to her friends. Mass emotions are aroused.

The other shoppers crowd eagerly around. No one now doubts that Joe is really guilty.

The people have become a mob, following ir-
responsible leaders. Students often point out
the analogy between this type of mob reaction and that of a nation like Nazi Germany.

Craving satisfaction for its blood lust, the mob batters the jail door with a telephone pole. Students begin to understand the lengths to which a mob will go when aroused.

The mob fires the jail. A ringleader flings dynamite into the blazing mass. Realism is added with newsreel footage taken of mob reaction at an actual lynching in California.

Scenes like this heighten the emotional impact of the film, stimulate classroom discussion. Here, as Joe's agonized face appears at the jail window, lynchers watch with glee.

Part 4: FILMS FOR DEMOCRACY

No one who has seen the documentary Air Forces film, *The Memphis Belle*, can forget the look on the pilot's sweat-streaked face as he guides his big bomber through flak "thick enough to walk on."

There was no love interest in that scene, no set other than the interior of a Flying Fortress with a bellyful of bombs. There were no women in the picture, no professional actors. Yet the film was a hit, and many people went to see it several times.

In motion picture history, *The Memphis Belle* may prove a landmark as important as David Wark Griffith's *The Birth of a Nation*, which is credited with starting the feature picture cycle. For *The Memphis Belle*, and other factual war films, may mark the coming of age of the documentary, both as a unit in itself and as raw material for parts of entertainment films.

Before the war, documentaries were regarded with reservations. They were made but not widely shown. *The Plow That Broke the Plains*, by Pare Lorentz, was admired by a few but it never was nationally released in commercial theaters. *The River*, also by Lorentz, was seen by only a fraction of the nation's theater-goers. The tendency was to dismiss documentary films as stodgy.

Now Hollywood has learned from films like *The Memphis Belle* that fact can be fully as exciting on the screen as fiction, fully as rich in the entertainment values which bring people to box-offices on Broadway and Main Street—and on Shanghai's Big Horse Road and Les Grandes Boulevards in Paris.

There is another reason to believe that documentaries may have achieved new and lasting vigor. Working in or for government agencies or the armed forces, many moviemakers have experimented with new ways of dramatizing facts and documenting ideas. Some of them have been under fire, have seen men suffer and die. Such experiences will almost certainly influence their future thoughts and plans.

Colonel Darryl Zanuck, for example, after filming the North African campaign, went back to Hollywood to produce *Wilson*, to plan for screening Wendell Willkie's book, *One World*, and to hire Louis de Rochemont, long the producer of *The March of Time*. Zanuck set him to work on *Fighting Lady*, the story of an aircraft carrier, which is told with the aid of five reels of actual battle film.

These and other signposts point to a cycle of more serious, more factual motion pictures. Now Hollywood, with world-wide markets soon to be reopened, with its new documentary techniques and growing maturity of thought, is in a position to seize an exciting opportunity—the opportunity to carry abroad the message of democracy and, at home, to help American audiences preserve belief in democratic principles.

Even before the war, films had already done much to help Americans, as well as foreigners, know and value the American heritage. When Cecil B. DeMille, as editor for the film industry, prepared *Land of Liberty*, a two-hour film cavalcade of American history, he found in 124 previously-released films scenes which, when clipped and put together, outlined the whole great story of how men and women came to the American wilderness, won a continent, and built a nation. Intended originally for showing at the New York World's Fair, *Land of Liberty* was later released in theaters throughout the country. Not a single scene had to be photographed especially for the picture.

But historical films were sometimes inaccurate. Treatments of American life were sometimes trivial or misleading. With its new war-born knowledge of the motion picture's power, filmdom probably will be careful to avoid such faults in the future.

In America, films can help to combat threats to democratic institutions and liberties. Abroad, they can help build a positive picture of friendly, powerful, democratic America. The following pages indicate what the American film has achieved in the past as an interpreter and champion of freedom and democracy. They also suggest what it may achieve in this role in the post-war world.

The motion picture industry has fully recognized its wartime responsibility. It has helped to win the war. It can help to win the peace.

"Equal justice under law," chiselled on the United States Supreme Court Building, expresses a cherished American ideal. Motion pictures can make such democratic ideals more real and dearer to an audience of millions in America and throughout the world.

Descendants of these early American "Commandos" (Rogers' Rangers in *Northwest Passage*) fight today in Jap-infested jungles.

Films have shown, and can continue to show, struggles of Americans, from pioneer days to the present, to win and maintain freedom.

Motion pictures have recreated scenes of hardship and adventure in the epic building of the American nation. Above, the pioneers move west in *Frontiersman*. Such films stimulate pride in our past, give us the perspective for better understanding of the present.

Here Raymond Massey, as Lincoln in the famous debate with Douglas, says, "This nation cannot exist half slave and half free." Pictures like *Abe Lincoln in Illinois* have reminded us that a nation which was conceived in liberty must cherish and extend it.

In this scene of the railroad's completion ceremony from *Union Pacific*, Leland Stanford misses golden spike with silver-tipped hammer. The $86,000 cost for research on this film shows how studios rival museums and libraries as custodians of Americana.

Thomas Edison's Menlo Park Laboratory, above, was reproduced in exact detail for *Edison the Man*, starring Spencer Tracy. The picture is one of a series of biographical films about the lives of great men, showing the United States as a land of opportunity.

The Story of Dr. Carver paid tribute to the great Negro scientist, born a slave, who added $60,000,000 a year to the South's income from experiments which created over 350 products from the peanut. Such films also can be useful in fighting race prejudice.

This scene from George Gershwin's popular *Porgy and Bess,* with all-Negro cast, was included in *Rhapsody in Blue,* a film version of Gershwin's life. Many motion pictures have reminded U. S. and foreign audiences of the Negro's contribution to American life.

Leopold Stokowski, above, has helped spread an appreciation of American culture by putting the world's greatest music on film sound-tracks. His pictures include *Fantasia* and *Christmas, 1944,* made by the Army for showings to American servicemen overseas.

Screen portrayals of great literary figures of the past have familiarized us with our country's intellectual history, reminding us that the motion picture is a record as well as a symbol of American culture. Above is Fredric March in the role of Mark Twain.

This scene, known as Lou Gehrig's farewell, is from *Pride of the Yankees*, starring Gary Cooper, which illustrated on the screen America's love of good sportsmanship. When Cooper entertained U.S. troops overseas, they often requested him to repeat the scene.

In this scene from *The River*, government-produced documentary, the camera was focused on soil erosion, pointing up the need for reforestation and flood control. Such films have shown how effectively motion pictures can help to visualize the tasks before us.

Massive dams of the TVA system, also pictured in *The River*, prevent ruinous floods, furnish power for industry, make possible cheap fertilizer for denuded lands. Thus, in striking appeals to eye and ear, films can present both a problem and its remedies.

Juvenile delinquency has received forthright film treatment in *Dead End, Boys' Town,* and the March of Time's *Youth in Crisis,* from which the scene above is taken. Other pressing social problems have been tackled with equal vigor and candor on the screen.

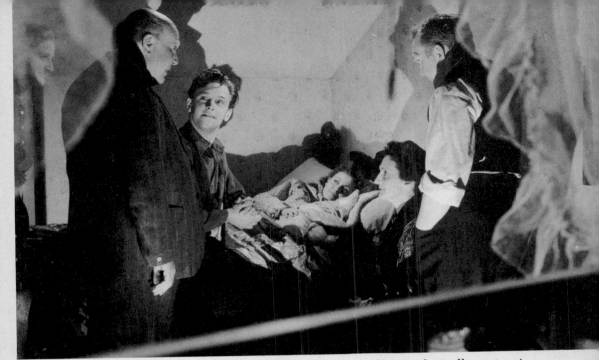

Above is a scene from *Our Town*, one of many films dealing with American family life. The Hardy and Aldrich family pictures are also among films realistically portraying the joys, sorrows and problems of the American home, the basic unit in our way of life.

The church, along with the American home and the public school, has provided background material for serious motion picture studies. This scene from *One Foot in Heaven* shows how a free pulpit aids in the unending struggle to maintain our democracy.

This newsreel shot was included in *Land of Liberty*, which reminded audiences of America's past. It shows Chief Justice Hughes addressing a joint session of Congress at a ceremony which commemorated the 150th anniversary of the U. S. Constitution. Sum-

marizing the basic concept of American democracy, the Chief Justice said: "The firmest ground for confidence in the future is that more than ever we realize that, while democracy must have its organization and its control, its vital breath is individual liberty."

We are indebted to the following sources for the pictures used in this book:

Acme

Lucien Aigner—Look

Artkino

Jules Buck—Modern Screen

British Combine

British Information Services .

Robert Capa—Pix Inc.

Capitol Pictures Corp.

Columbia Pictures

Culver

Walt Disney Studios

European

Farm Security Administration

Federal Bureau of Investigation

Fox Movietone News

Philip Gendreau

Sam Goldwyn Studios

Bob Hansen

Harris and Ewing

Joe Heppner

Dr. Ernst Herz

Intercontinents

International News Photo

Thomas Kwang—Paul Guillumette

Bob Leavitt

March of Time

Peter Martin

Metro-Goldwyn-Mayer

John Mills, Jr.

Movieland Magazine

Museum of Modern Art

National Broadcasting Company

National Film Board of Canada

News of the Day

Newsphotos

N.Y.U. Film Library

OEM Defense Photos

Alexander Paal

Paramount Pictures

Pathe News

Penguin Photos

Pictures Inc.

PM

Press Association

R.K.O.

Harold Rhodenbaugh—Look

Russell Birdwell Office

Bob Sandberg—Look

Sovfoto

John Swope—Random House, Inc.

Standard Oil Company of New Jersey

Maurice Terrell—Look

Earl Theisen—Look

20th Century-Fox

Union Pacific Railroad

United Artists

U.S. Army Air Forces

U.S. Army Signal Corps

U.S. Coast Guard

U.S. Marine Corps

U.S. Navy

U.S.O. Camp Shows

Bob Wallace

War Activities Committee

Warner Bros.

Len Weissman—Motion Picture Magazine

Wright Aeronautical Corp.

Wide World